Dora B

Dora B
a memoir of my mother

Josiane Behmoiras

VIKING
an imprint of
PENGUIN BOOKS

VIKING

Published by the Penguin Group
Penguin Group (Australia)
250 Camberwell Road, Camberwell, Victoria 3124, Australia
(a division of Pearson Australia Group Pty Ltd)
Penguin Group (USA) Inc.
375 Hudson Street, New York, New York 10014, USA
Penguin Group (Canada)
90 Eglinton Avenue East, Suite 700, Toronto, ON M4P 2Y3, Canada
(a division of Pearson Canada Inc.)
Penguin Books Ltd
80 Strand, London WC2R 0RL, England
Penguin Ireland
25 St Stephen's Green, Dublin 2, Ireland
(a division of Penguin Books Ltd)
Penguin Books India Pvt Ltd
11 Community Centre, Panchsheel Park, New Delhi – 110 017, India
Penguin Group (NZ)
Cnr Airborne and Rosedale Roads, Albany, Auckland, New Zealand
(a division of Pearson New Zealand Ltd)
Penguin Books (South Africa) (Pty) Ltd
24 Sturdee Avenue, Rosebank, Johannesburg 2196, South Africa

Penguin Books Ltd, Registered Offices: 80 Strand, London WC2R 0RL, England

First published by Penguin Group (Australia), a division of
Pearson Australia Group Pty Ltd, 2005

1 3 5 7 9 10 8 6 4 2

Text copyright © Josiane Behmoiras, 2005

The moral right of the author has been asserted

All rights reserved. Without limiting the rights under copyright reserved above, no part of this publication may be reproduced, stored in or introduced into a retrieval system, or transmitted, in any form or by any means (electronic, mechanical, photocopying, recording or otherwise), without the prior written permission of both the copyright owner and the above publisher of this book.

Cover and text design by Debra Billson © Penguin Group (Australia)
Cover image of pomegranates, bug and limbs by Jo Whaley/Getty Images;
Hissing Cockroach/Getty Images
Author photograph by Vicky Bell
Typeset in 12.5/18.5 pt Perpetua by Post Pre-press Group, Brisbane, Queensland
Printed in Australia by McPherson's Printing Group Pty Ltd, Maryborough, Victoria

National Library of Australia
Cataloguing-in-Publication data:

Behmoiras, Josiane, 1953– .
Dora B: a memoir of my mother

ISBN 0 670 02865 7.

1. Behmoiras, Dora. 2. Mothers and daughters. 3. Mother and child.
4. Mothers – Biography. I. title.

www.penguin.com.au

This project has been assisted by the Commonwealth Government through the Arts Council,
its arts funding and advisory body.

To my daughter,
with love

> *Le Meunier repartit:*
> *'Je suis âne, il est vrai, j'en conviens, je l'avoue;*
> *Mais que dorénavant on me blâme, on me loue,*
> *Qu'on dise quelque chose ou qu'on ne dise rien,*
> *J'en veux faire à ma tête.' Il le fit, et fit bien.*

'Ass! ass!' the miller replied; 'we're asses three!
I do avow myself an ass to be;
But since my sage advisers can't agree,
Their words henceforth shall not be heeded;
I'll suit myself.' And he succeeded.

from *'Le Meunier, Son Fils et l'Ane'*,
Jean de la Fontaine, 1621–1695

My mother wakes up in the middle of the night, rolls over until her shoes touch the ground, grabs her handbag, which doubles as her pillow, and out of it produces a fold-up clock and a broken biscuit. She opens the clock, presses a button to illuminate the time, then closes the clock and puts it back in her bag. She eats the biscuit for her midnight snack, wiping the crumbs from her mouth, then gets up from her bench and walks across the small square on King Saul Street until she reaches a telephone booth at the edge of a deserted footpath. Out of her handbag she takes a magnetic plastic card, puts it into the slot and with her finger composes a long number she has stored in her head.

In Australia it's eight o'clock in the morning when the telephone rings. My daughter rushes to the phone, like children often do. As soon as she has answered the call she waves both arms, one holding a peanut-butter toast and the other holding the receiver, which she hands to me as if it were a hot brick. I immediately know it's my mother calling and I brace myself for the usual shriek, '*Allô, allô!*

C'est toi, ma fille?' I will reply with a feeble *'Oui maman, c'est moi'* – I call her *maman*, but I think of her as Dora, not as my mother. I will hold the receiver away from my head, letting her curse this or that enemy, keep silent and hear nothing but from time to time her voice calling, *'Allô, allô,'* can you hear me?' I will answer *'Oui, maman,'* and listen to the crooked fan creaking inside our gas heater, the news from around Australia coming from the radio, the old man next door whistling in his back yard, teaching his budgerigar the same old song that the bird won't sing.

But this time, as soon as I take the receiver I sense distress in the familiar forceful tone. Dora's voice is shakier than usual. *'Ma fille,* oh, you don't know what happened to me!'

'What, *maman?'* I am alarmed.

'They have stolen my suitcase,' she says.

'Where, how did it happen?'

'Yesterday, on the beach,' she says in an apologetic voice, as if she had been frivolous. 'I was tired; the suitcase was heavy with all my belongings in it.'

I am angry with her for carrying a suitcase instead of wheeling a jeep. 'The cursed thieves! Now I have nothing left.' Her voice is trembling but she doesn't cry. 'I pulled the suitcase and then I sat on the beach, my back against it. I fell asleep. I woke up sleeping on the sand and it was gone.'

All I can say is *'Oh, maman . . .'*

'Don't worry, my darling,' she says. 'I will get another suitcase and fill it up again. *Allô, allô,* do you hear me?' Dora checks that I am still on the line, still listening, before continuing with her monologue of rage. 'The cursed thieves! My stolen possessions will bring them bad luck, amen!'

'*Oui,*' I answer, for lack of other words.

'Now listen, you have to help me. Did you do what I told you?' Her voice recovers; she is back to her normal tone. On and on she will go, begging me to write to this or that world leader to ask for help, and as always I am already escaping. I revisit the beach in Tel-Aviv I saw twelve years ago. She would have gone there in the late afternoon, it would be too hot during the day under the harsh sun of August. By now most of the bathers would be home, cool, showered, sitting on their balconies in clean white cotton vests, careful with the juice of their fresh watermelon. The air on the beach would be still and warm. The sun would be descending on the water, tilting the atmosphere toward melancholy. Maybe a few girls in bikinis would still be lying on colourful beach towels licking icy-poles, and one or two hopeful young males would be making passes at them: 'Excuse me, I think I know you from somewhere, did you ever work at the Discount Bank?' The echo of a rubber ball thudding between two wooden rackets would fill the temporary silence of the day's end, two pairs of feet running on the edge of the water where the sand is firmer. My mother would enter that scene dragging a heavy suitcase, stopping and starting again, undecided about the best spot to have a rest; leaving behind her an uneven groove in the sand, her suitcase resisting the pull of her eighty-five-year-old hands.

'*Allô*, are you there?'

'*Oui*,' I answer.

'Did you hear what I said?'

'What . . .'

'*Ecoute!*' she says. 'Listen carefully to what you have to do. Listen, this time. You have to ask your husband to ring Bill Clinton. I sent a letter to Bill Clinton. He knows all about you. All, all. He is a kind man and he understands my case. He will help me and all and all. *Allô*, are you there?

'Clinton will like your husband, they will be friends, you will see. *Allô*? Let me talk to your hus—' beep beep beep beep beep . . . It's my sound of salvation. Her credit is consumed and I hang up. She will clench the plastic card in her hand as she walks back to her bench. She will sit down under the shadow of a twenty-storey building, eat another biscuit and look up, knowing that only the sky is her limit. She won't give up the Clinton idea. Not just yet.

It eases my mind, knowing she is already recovering

from this latest loss of her belongings, back on her usual quest for the attention of world leaders.

I can imagine her walking along the affluent streets of Tel-Aviv, holding a letter addressed to François Mitterand or to Queen Elizabeth. Her hair matted, her clothes mismatched layers, crumpled and stained dresses, shirts, cardigan, coats. Two pairs of looking glasses are held together with string; one eye blind, cloudy, the other in need of a thicker lens. Her face tense with confusion and her step heavy with exhaustion. Her skin diseased from lack of washing.

But sometimes I see her the way she was in those warm summers of bliss. If I try hard, I can picture her standing in a creek, her body illuminated by the first light of morning. She is bowing to scoop me from the water. I let go of a snail and she lifts me high above the stream. My head is nestling against the curve of her neck and I inhale her freshness. I wrestle with my memory to catch a glimpse of the butterflies and dragonflies that used to fly around her, gleaming against the shade of the blackberry bushes. I know the name of that place. The word is warm and velvety in my mouth, like my mother's breasts when they were full of milk: Chevreuse.

I have a black-and-white photo taken in 1955.

My mother is smiling, in a floral bikini-top teamed

with pinstriped, cuffed shorts. She is kneeling at my side, her two tanned arms wrapped around me, her fingers interlaced against my waist. I am three years old, frowning under the sun in pointy straw hat and polkadot bloomers. We are posing outside our twin-peak tent, by the pine tree. She chose this spot to pitch her tent when she first brought me to Chevreuse, as a newborn, when she put my pram under the branches, my head in the shade and my legs in the sun. She would return to this same spot every summer.

In the background are the tents of other campers. I stare at the photo for a long time, until I see people emerging from under the canvas, walking towards us. My mother gets up, takes my hand and we follow a group of campers on a path bordered by the grass – I can hear the crickets. We keep going, past the reception windows – from where Madame Isblé is no doubt peering, guarding her abundant apple trees – and out under the gate of the camping grounds, with two giant wooden cartwheels, one on each side. Along the country road bordered by the never-ending woods we sing and step, left right, left right, past the pink foxgloves at the fringe of the woods, which seem to be growing tall like trees. Left, right, left, right, and off to the right follow the path, children stomping on the white gravel. We have arrived at the *fruitière*; I don't notice that we have passed the wishing well, and find a coin is stuck against my sweaty palm – I have forgotten to make a wish. We are already inside the stone building and Dora is giving me a pear.

'*Beraha i salud,*' my mother might have said in her own language, a blessing for good health, relishing the sight of pear juice running down her granddaughter's chin, cutting crooked pieces of fruit with a paring knife. But she never saw my daughter as a little girl – now a twelve-year-old who will one day ask for an explanation. I will have to tell her that her grandmother is a baglady. But there is more to be said about Dora. Stories about a poinciana tree instead of a roof, meat instead of roses, fish stories, wolf stories, garlic, lupin and sour sauce, pomegranate juice for blood clotting, a needle stitching chicken skin or a bride's veil – a long string of stories that are mine as much as hers.

And there is another story. It was said that Dora's grandmother uttered a dreadful malediction, alone in the empty family house in Edirne, abandoned by her son. In 1925 my grandfather was taking his family to the enlightened city of Paris, away from the upheaval of looming war and the secular reforms of Atatürk, leaving my great-grandmother behind. Did she really curse her son Haim Behmoiras and his lineage for eternity?

Looking at the life of Dora, it is hard not to believe so.

France

The blue bear

One morning I wake up alone in the bed I share with my mother. On the windowsill sits my teddy bear dripping dark red, drying in the winter sun. My mother says she dyed the bear in Bordeaux because he was getting dirty, but I liked him better sky-blue, the way I received him from my uncle Sammy.

My mother says, 'My brother, he is cross with me. He didn't want you to arrive.'

My uncle Sammy comes to our small room on rue de la Croix Nivert with bags of toys and clothes from his shops. She watches him put a shoe on my foot, do up the buckle and say, 'This one is too small' or 'This one is way too big' or 'This one is just big enough, with some room for growth.'

The paw-print

I see the muddy paw of a dog imprinted on a white cloth my mother has spread on the ground. I hear my mother shriek '*Oh! Le chien!*' But the dog is quick to disappear into the crowd. My mother freezes in time surrounded by old wares and rusty bits of metal, chipped porcelain, musty wood, faded cloth and the echoes of talking, announcing, arguing and singing in the Sunday flea market of Porte de Vanves. For a moment I think she is going to cry. But she doesn't. She just stands there gazing at the horizon, ignoring the muddy paw-print and the messed-up merchandise on the white canvas at her feet.

We have collected these things together early in the mornings under the ultramarine sky of Paris, blowing steam into the cold air. We sneaked into the courtyards of rich people, lifted the lids of rubbish bins and found our treasures: a bunch of wilted pink artificial flowers, a white embroidered tablecloth speckled with rust, a man's shirt marked with red lipstick, a satin purse coming undone at the seam. We carried our treasures from the back courtyard, tiptoeing on white marble, running past the large French window behind which sits the concierge, and if Dora giggled I whispered 'Shhhh'. Back in our room, she reshaped the flowers, stitched the purse, washed and ironed the clothes in our tiny kitchen.

My mother eventually bends down and lifts the corner of the white cloth and shakes the mud away as best as she can, without tipping her merchandise, then rearranges the display. The paw-print is still there, stamped on her white canvas, but she ignores it. She smiles at passers-by, hoping to sell something so she can buy me a newspaper cone of French fries for my lunch.

At lunchtime, I eat my hot chips standing by the stall next to ours. I see an old lady in a wheelchair, selling her tortoiseshell cat. She is talking to the cat. 'You know I am going to die, so it would not be fair if you were to bear me a grudge for selling you.'

She kisses the cat a few more times, before she hands him to his new owner. My mother doesn't see the selling of the cat, because again she is staring into the distance. Although I am only four years old, I see her despair.

Gleaning

Dora is hiding in the darkness behind the staircase, inside the entrance of an apartment building, checking the satin pocket of her girdle where she keeps her notes. Her face darkens.

'We are broke,' she says. She rearranges her stockings, fumbling with the rubber buttons of her suspenders, and sighs. 'Come on. Let us go and find some food.'

The sellers are packing up as we walk along the stalls.

'It won't be long,' says Dora. After the market finishes we are allowed to pick fruits and vegetables from the floor.

But I have spotted red cherries under one of the trestle tables. I crawl and pluck a punnet out of a full box. Nobody notices. But Dora has seen me, and she frowns at my loot.

'We are not thieves, you know. We can only pick what has been thrown onto the floor. This time I'll let you keep them because I can't take cherries out of a child's hand. But don't do this ever again.'

Dr Godot

The bell rings inside the apartment on Rue de la Convention. Dora rushes to the double carved doors, but I stand in her way. I won't let Dr Godot in. I am very cross with him for what he has done. Dora has said to him, '*Oh, là là, docteur,* there is no need to make a drama about your wallpaper, and anyway the pattern is so busy you can't even see the scribbles.' But he got even angrier and threw down my doll and her head broke and rolled on the parquet floor, her eyes closing and opening. Then he stormed out to have his dinner at the restaurant.

Dora manages to open the door but I slam it closed. She opens it again and there is Dr Godot sitting on the stairs, saying to me, 'All right then, I will stay here, on the stairs.' He looks so sad and lonely and old that I feel sorry for him and let him in.

He puts his feet on giant green felt skaters and glides left and right, left and right on the parquetry that my mother has polished with beeswax. He retires to his room on the far right and we go to the opposite side, on the far left. Dora unrolls our mattress on the kitchen floor, and we lower ourselves into bed. The last thing I see before I close my eyes is the wooden shelf loaded with five china jars, aligned by order of size, containing remains from the times Madame Godot was still alive. Inside the biggest jar is a layer of hardened yellow flour. The next, marked '*Sucre*', is empty because I licked the leftovers. Then there is dusty tea, an odourless brown slab of coffee, a shimmering of salt. When we moved here, Dr Godot warned my mother not to clean the jars. He says they are his memories.

In the hall the dry wood of the clock is creaking as the pendulum swings left and right, tic-toc.

My mother rises early in the morning and boils the kettle. Then screams emerge from the kitchen.

'*Docteur, docteur*, help me! Oh, my daughter!'

Dr Godot enters our kitchen only in times of disaster. Not long ago Dora accidentally broke a window, and in her nonchalance left the glass shards lying on top of the open dustbin in the passageway. I passed by the bin and my bare leg was slashed by the sharp glass, drawing a thick line of blood. Dr Godot was quick with Mercurochrome and bandages. Before that, it was soapy water that Dora had splashed on the linoleum that made me skid and hurt my head against the stove. On this morning she has tripped over the mattress and spilt boiling water from the kettle over my arm. The doctor is rushing towards the kitchen, gliding on his giant green felt skaters, leaving them behind when he steps on the kitchen linoleum.

'Calm down, Dora, please!'

He is spreading an ointment, which oozes like honey out of a little tube onto my scalded flesh. I am glad it's not Mitosyl – that ointment stinks of fish.

'What's that ointment?' asks Dora. 'I use Mitosyl, it's far superior,' she adds, frowning.

Dr Godot nods and wraps my arm with white gauze, then vanishes back to his corner room. Later, Dora unwraps the gauze from my arm and gets me to sit by the window, turning my arm to expose the scalded skin to the sun.

At ten o'clock exactly we are sitting by the entrance, Dora and I. The door is ajar, a fraction of the staircase showing and the security chain in place.

'I am watching,' says Dora, 'I am watching for an Algerian. They are everywhere, they hurt people all over Paris. Sooner or later an Algerian could come and get us here.'

I am watching the void of the stairwell. As I have been doing every morning, for hours and for days and months, anticipating the loud steps, the heavy breath, the dreaded giant body bobbing up from behind the landing, confident that Dora would slam the door in time to save us from its claws.

Not many people ring our bell. Dora says that Dr Godot doesn't have many patients because a lot of them have died, and the new generation don't want to have their heartbeat checked through a small wooden funnel. 'No wonder. We are in the modern times!' she says.

While Dora dusts the tails of dragons on tall Chinese vases and the claws of beasts on armchairs in the large salon, I recite children's words she has written for me: *caca, pipi tata, toutou, coco, dodo, lolo, bébé, mémé*. She tells everybody, 'My daughter is only five but she can read.' She buys me picture books with gold bindings, a miniature pram, and many dolls. On Sundays she takes me to the *Guignol* puppet show in the Jardins du Luxembourg and buys me ice-cream and cakes. She sends me to school but I don't like it, so against the rules she keeps me at home.

One day the doorbell interrupts the silence of the afternoon. Dora engages the security chain and opens the door a fraction.

'Madame Behmoiras?'

'*Oui*,' she replies.

She closes the door to release the chain and then opens it again. A man is standing there, wearing a grey dustcoat. He hands his notebook to Dora, with a pen. She signs her name in running writing and takes the telegram. I expect exciting news but as Dora opens the folded paper and reads, her face shrinks with despair.

'Sammy, Sammy, my brother Sam . . .'

Dora has pinned a black mourning ribbon around the sleeve of her tailored jacket.

'A heart attack, that's impossible. Sixty-five is not that old. Two brothers and two sisters and my mother and father I lost in Paris. They are all in the sky. And the sky is always grey in Paris,' she says as she folds clothes into a suitcase.

'And the Algerian. There is always the Algerian who could come one day and get us, pretend to be a patient, and when I open the door . . . *Non, non!*'

Our suitcase and tent are at the door. We are going to Chevreuse, as we do every summer, but I know something is wrong. Dr Godot is sitting by his mahogany piano, his back to the ivory and ebony keys, crying.

'Don't go, Dora, don't go. Where will I find another honest employee like you? Why don't you wait? One of these days I will retire, and there will be a place for you two in Lyon, with my family.'

But Dora won't listen.

Dr Godot looks sad and lonely. That's how I will remember him, me very young and him very, very old, waiting for us to return.

Slippery fish

It's our last summer in the valley of Chevreuse. Opalescent dragonflies are purring at the creek while women sing their songs with water dancing around their legs. We walk along the country road bordered by the woods, see the reflection of wrought iron breaking on the dark water when a coin is thrown into the well. The old *fruitière* building is dense with the cider-sharp mustiness of sweet apples and pears. The days are shortening and the creek is swelling with icy water; campers are folding up their tents; cars roll away, gravel flying, through the heavy gate with the two cartwheels, which Madame Isblé closes on the empty camp. Dora and I hitch a ride to the village in one of the cars; she sells our tent, folding the notes into her purse and then taking them out again to hand to an old man as payment for a room in his house where we will spend our first autumn in Chevreuse.

The old man is pushing me in a wheelbarrow over a narrow bridge across the river, pretending to tip me into the water. The water reflects the sun onto the red and yellow leaves dangling from a roof against the dark old laundry shed. Last week my mother was kneeling under this roof, immersing a cloth in the river, slapping it against the serrated plank, singing with the other women from the camping grounds the song of the Portuguese washerwomen: 'Slap and slap harder, sleep better tonight.' Now Dora is sleeping off her illness behind our bedroom door as the old man cuts pieces of stale bread with his opinel knife, drops them into my bowl of salty vegetable soup and says, 'You don't drink water while you eat your soup!' A long afternoon in the old man's enclosed *potager*, the ground underneath me throbbing with the weak thumps of his pickaxe turning the soil to plant leeks and potatoes for his winter soups.

Dora is on her feet again, all dressed up in her white lace shirt, fresh and soft like a peach, smiling at a real-estate agent as we enter an old house in the village. We are standing inside on the ground floor, but there is no floor. The wood is rotten; the cellar is showing through the beams and the real-estate agent says, 'It can be fixed.' Dora nods and answers, 'Yes, it can be fixed.'

In the winter, Dora searches for a refuge from town to town, in Rambouillet, in Fontainebleau, under the wet trees on the wet streets of forgotten towns where at dusk women close all the wooden shutters of their houses. I want to return to Dr Godot, but she says, *'Paris, c'est fini!'*

'Where are we going, *maman?*' I ask her.

'I don't know,' she answers. 'Maybe south, where it's much warmer.'

I hold her hand and walk the distances, my body on a new mattress every night. At the age of six I have grown tired of being little Josiane. One rainy afternoon I find who I want to be in a train station enveloped with the silence of plants, flowers, shrubs and small trees. The station is deserted as our train enters. I see two old fountains, one marked *'Eau potable'* the other marked *'Eau non potable'* on rusty signs. We get off the train and Dora makes me drink from the fountain of drinkable water, lifting me up to reach the tap. As she wipes my mouth with the tip of her scarf, I notice the passengers getting out of another empty carriage. They are two jovial women with abundant grey hair and wrinkles on their faces, wearing dark rain jackets and rubber boots. They look quite similar, and in my memory I will never be able to tell one from the other. The first is free of any luggage; the second is carrying a big old canvas bag, the weight of which seems to make her bend. They walk to the creaking scales positioned by the wall and the one holding the bag produces a big dead fish, slippery and shiny, and puts it on the tray.

They shout and laugh. 'It's the biggest ever,' says one, and the other answers, 'My word it is!'

They giggle with pleasure and look again at the scales

before putting the fish back in the bag and walking out of the station. I want to leave my shell behind, be no more who I am. I want to skip the years of my life like a hopscotch game, to get quickly to the end. To be one of the two old ladies, and Dora the other. We would go to our home and share the fish by the wood fire.

Rolling coin

We travel south. After a long voyage we arrive one night in the train station of Montpellier, Dora and I and one suitcase, in 1959.

We are starting anew. Deserted streets, brown leaves flying in the wind, light filtering through the curtains, houses where people live. I imagine Dr Godot still sitting by his mahogany piano, waiting for us to return. My mother tugs my hand and we keep walking, looking for a room in the foreign city. Dora empties her vinyl purse on the reception desk of a hotel. In the morning, I whimper as she pulls my hair, combing it in a rush. By ten o'clock we have to leave the room. 'It's the rule,' she says.

I see the pale yellow walls of a partition; they do not reach the ceiling and this room stays open even when our door is closed. From above a smell of perfume is drifting in; it must be the sweet Russian refugee with her cheeks shiny from oil and red from rouge. She is returning from her promenade before the gates close for the night. I hear the soft snoring of a child and the shy coughing of an old woman. I hear the heartbeat of my mother. We are squeezed together in a single bed, Dora and I. The Salvation Army hostel is full tonight and we share our room with a young woman. When she changes into her nightgown on my bed across the room, I stare at her enormous breasts. She covers herself with her crossed arms and says to Dora, 'Can you tell your daughter to close her eyes while I undress?'

Dora has been hired as a maid; she makes up the beds of people who sleep in their ancestors' luxury of lace and carved wood. She says the Salvation Army refuge is not our future. It is true, our room is musty, cold and bare, but it's located next to the homestead's kitchen garden. I spend my days enclosed by the stone walls of the *potager*, playing with the pliable, moist soil. A boy my age dressed in brown corduroy pants enters my garden; he stares at me with disdain. ''Tis not yours, the garden,' he says. 'Get out of here!'

I need not worry about my situation, because my mother is dismissed from her new job. The two of us are soon back on the road, under the brilliant sky. The crickets sing their summer song. Dora's voice shakes with every step.

'The bastards, it's *them*. They are following me around and they force everyone to show me the door.'

On the old building there is a roof and on the roof there is a room; inside the room a wide bed and in the bed are Dora and I. She reads to me every night from a picture book with golden binding. She says, 'They like their *morue à la parmentier,* Monsieur and Madame Féral, I cook it for them nearly every day.' But Dora knows what I like best. She has made a wick by braiding cotton strings, pierced a hole in the lid of a closed biscuit tin to thread the wick through, and filled the base of the tin with alcohol to feed the flame. She props a small saucepan on that tin lid with three flat pebbles she has collected from the river. She boils water and cooks noodles on her makeshift stove, seasons them with a knob of butter so that I'll devour them. The neighbour from the adjacent roof calls out 'Josiane!' Over the low wall she hands me a doughnut for my dessert. Shame that Monsieur and Madame Féral have to go into a home, or so I have heard.

Dora enrols me in school in the middle of the year, and although I have been reading since the age of four I can't follow the lesson from the back of the classroom, where I have been seated. The teacher, dressed in her grey dustcoat, frowns at me from the podium, saying, 'Stand up please, and give us the answer.' But I don't know the question.

'A sausage,' I say, angry.

The whole class laughs. 'Ha-ha,' they say, 'a sausage in a bathtub!'

At the end of school my mother is waiting outside, hiding something behind her back. It's a surprise for me, a pair of metal roller-skates.

The soup of wild leeks bubbles on the stove; Dora is stirring the pot in the green kitchen of a man called Joe. I like dinnertime, when I roll the three green-checked serviettes into the wooden rings and put them on the table, one for each of us. Dora is gracious with the ladle, saying '*Voilà*' and giggling in anticipation of praise as Joe empties his glass of wine. The leeks, which we have picked from vineyards along the road, make delicious soup mopped up with a crusty slice of white bread. Dora shakes the crumbs into the sink and puts the tablecloth back on the table, straightening with her hand imaginary crinkles, watching Joe drink another bottle. He gets out his wooden pendulum and a pair of scissors. He points a blade above a map of greater Montpellier with one hand, holding the string in his other hand and watching the pendulum slowly swing. With every swing, the blade descends onto the map, until its point touches the paper. 'That's where she is, that's where the missing woman is, her body is rotting in the ground,' he says and Dora mumbles, 'Please, Joe, the child.'

His fingers are curling against his palm, he slams the table. 'The child, the child . . . she always says "No", your child, *hein* . . . your stubborn child.'

My mother shelters me from him with her body. He gets up, wobbles closer raising his fist at me, but he is too slow. She drags me into my bedroom and turns the key in the lock. She holds me tight in my narrow bed.

'Don't worry, *chérie*, in the morning we will leave.'

My favourite thing about the ground-floor room is the floral wallpaper. Are they yellow lilies? They turn golden when the morning sun glows on the wall. But Dora says the landlady's children told her off for renting the spare room to us. Aren't parents the ones that are meant to do the telling-off?

My few toys are piled in my doll's pram. The pram is in the middle of the paved courtyard; we can't take it with us. A neighbour's girl, about my age, is standing at a distance. As we walk away she pounces on the pram and wheels it to her place in a hurry, my toys rattling away from me. Dora, with our suitcase in one hand, puts her arm around my shoulder and gently turns my head the other way. '*Ma pauvre chérie*,' she says.

In a quiet street a man is driving his Citroën Deux Chevaux into his garage. Before he can pull the roller-door right down, Dora rushes at him.

'Please, Monsieur, can we sleep in your car? Just for the night, we have been walking all day, we are so tired.'

He refuses, and I like this man for the way he averts his eyes from Dora as he whispers a short '*Non*'.

The old wooden bench at the police station is hard under my body. We have been arrested for vagrancy while sitting on a park bench, our suitcase on the ground. My mother didn't have the one new franc required by law as proof that we weren't vagrants.

'Here, a coat for the little one.' A group of women inside a wire cage are all talking together. Each one of them is holding her fur coat and waving. One of the policemen opens the cage door with the big key dangling from his belt, and grabs two coats for me. Dora makes a bed on the wooden table, she tucks me in the perfumed fur.

'Why are they in a cage, *maman*?' I ask.

'Because they are "hens",' my mother says.

'What are hens?'

'Bad women,' Dora mumbles.

It's a pleasant train ride — wooden carriages, brass shelves and a steaming locomotive. We are moving so slowly on the narrow rails that you could jump off and walk alongside the carriage, pick some poppies or daisies and hop back on. At the end of the line, the small town of Palavas-les-Flots is fresh with the smell of fish and seaweed carried on the cold sea breeze. At the Monoprix Dora buys a brown Christmas carrybag filled with roasted chicken, pâté and crunchy mini-toasts, a loaf of honey cake, a checked cotton tea-towel. She finds a hotel room, spreads the tea-towel on the floor, arranges the food on it and says we are having a picnic. She washes our clothes with soap in the oval sink, and steam rises from my patched trousers strung over the radiator.

The next morning we wander the streets of Palavas in search of a new life. At the end of an empty day my mother takes me to the deserted beach. 'Where are we going, *maman*?' I ask her as we trudge with our suitcase in the fine sand under a cloudy sunset. 'Follow me, my darling, I know a place . . .'

The caravans look like giant snails. This one has no lock on it, and Dora opens it effortlessly. Inside, umbrellas, sand toys, beach mats and a giant inner tube, inflated plump, are waiting for the summer. Dora fills the hollow tube with folded canvas to make my bed. She uses her woollen coat to tuck me in. Outside the wind is howling, the sea is wild, but I feel safe with Dora sitting beside me on the floor. She writes a note of apology for the caravan's owners:

Please excuse us for using your caravan for shelter. I also found a coin of two new francs, and I kept it. I need it more than you do at present.

Regards, Dora.

'Sleep well,' she says, 'sleep well, my child, tomorrow will be a new day.'

Back in Montpellier there is no room for us in the Salvation Army hostel. Again, we sleep in the waiting-room of the railway station, with the passengers who are waiting for their morning train. Dora fears being arrested for vagrancy; she hasn't got a coin to show the police if they happen to turn up. Her face is strained as she asks the woman next to her for one new franc. The woman refuses, but in the early morning with her bones aching – unaccustomed to sleeping the night on a bench – she repents and offers the coin to my mother. Dora grabs it and in a fit of rage throws it back at the woman, saying, 'Here is your coin; bend down to pick it up!' The coin rolls away then spins round and round, back toward the woman, and with a last flutter falls face-down near her feet.

I see a coin rolling, forever rolling on a cold dirty floor.

Exile

One morning in the Montpellier police headquarters a detective is looking at my mother's proof of identity. A blue card that folds three times to form a booklet, it bears a stamped photo of Dora wearing pearl earrings and a lace collar, looking very young. The detective reads to himself: 'Turkish repatriate.'

'I have been in France for thirty-six years,' says Dora.

A second detective, standing by the desk, looks at the card. 'You are Jewish, aren't you?'

'Yes,' replies my mother, in a faint voice.

'*Alors*, the solution to your problem is simple.'

I hear him talking on the phone, emphasising some foreign words: *Jews, Is-ra-ël*. The other detective offers me a bonbon in a colourful wrapper. At the age of eight I have seen enough, and now my captor is pretending to be nice. My hands in my pocket, I hiss at him. 'Don't try to buy me with your sweets and your false smiles.'

He says nothing.

We are issued with two train tickets to Marseille. We are driven to the station in an unmarked police car, then escorted into our carriage. The two detectives watch until the train departs. The one who has offered me the lolly waves at me and I wave back, briefly. His lips are moving; I think he is saying *'Bon voyage'*.

We travel light, without luggage. I miss the suitcase we had to leave behind. The hotel owner confiscated it when Dora couldn't pay for an extra night, and so we slept in the station waiting-room and caught the attention of the police patrol because we didn't have a suitcase or one new franc. My school *tablier* was in it: the compulsory dustcoat my mother hand-stitched from raspberry-pink nylon cloth and trimmed with buttons in the shape of a pair of clogs. It was the nicest in the classroom. Dora laments the bundle of photos. I vaguely remember one that showed us standing among the pigeons of Sacré-Coeur. Was there a green ornamental metal fountain in that photo? Or maybe it's my memory of cool water splashing my white dress with the tartan trimming, and a matching tartan scarf you could loop for security through two buttonholes in the dress's collar.

We arrive in Marseille and report to the police station as instructed. We are sent to the Jewish Agency. We have to wait two months for the ship that will take us to The

Promised Land, as Dora calls that place. She doesn't like the transfer camp, with its lines of washing crisscrossing the huts and children running to look at us, so we take the bus back to town and check into the grand old building of the Salvation Army. We sleep in a big dormitory with the other women and children. At night a boy my age sits on his bed and yells loudly into the silence, 'It smells of Jews in here,' then pulls the covers over his face.

After a month as my schoolteacher, Madame Henry has grown fond of my mother and me. 'You don't belong to the Salvation Army,' she says, and takes us into her home. She makes a bed for her children on the lounge-room floor and gives us their small room. A wooden Jesus nailed onto a metal cross is hanging on the wall above my bed, watching over us. At night, Madame Henry makes me pray to Jesus for our safe voyage. 'He listens to people from all religions,' she says. She has collected gifts and clothes for us. Dora buys a suitcase to carry them.

The time to board our ship is nearing. At the Jewish Agency's dispensary a nurse scratches my arm with a quill and saturates the scratch with a transparent liquid. As the nurse turns to attend to the next person, Dora tries to wipe off the liquid with my coarse woollen cardigan. 'It's poison,' she whispers to me, but I jerk my arm away. The serum storms in, agitates my bloodstream, flushes me with a potent fever, and when I recover, I am immune to the ravages of smallpox. This is the last gift I carry away from my country of birth.

הֹוֶה

I have a photo of us taken in Marseille on a cloudy day. Dora is standing next to me on a wide footpath, and I am smiling, holding a white dove supplied by the photographer. Dora is leaning to one side to wrap her arm around my shoulder and her face is tight with the effort of a smile. Years later, in our asbestos hut in Israel, she will tell me she chose that photographer because of the white dove and her belief that it would bring some peace into our lives.

I am now holding the photo in the palm of my ageing hand and I know what our future was. I look at her in the photo and I say: *Don't go, Dora, don't go! You will regret it for the rest of your life if you go to Israel. Please, stay in Marseille.*

The Promised Land

Oranges

My mother lets go of my hand for a few seconds, just to bend over and apply her lips to the Israeli soil while other people keep walking ahead, oblivious to her gesture. Then she gets up, takes my hand again and carries her suitcase in the other hand. The sun caresses our faces on this mild Israeli winter day. We make our way with a group of other migrants to the pick-up truck, our feet searching for a new kind of balance on the hard ground of the port of Haifa.

For seven stormy days we have been tossed on the Mediterranean, the waves lifting, dropping, swaying our ship and making us yearn for land, any firm land. The migrants' quarters below deck have turned into a sea-sickness ward, with suppository wrappers rolling on the lavatory floor and hard-boiled eggs rolling about on plates in the deserted dining-room. Dora, who was not fazed by the storm, adopted that naughty expression that comes with giggling and a sense of adventure; together we climbed the stairs up to the deck, and the stewards – who were keeping the upper class strictly migrant-free – mistook us for tourists and offered us drinks.

'You see,' said Dora to me, 'I tell you, *we* are distinguished.'

She spent the afternoons chatting with the travellers, pretending we were on a pleasure cruise.

The pick-up truck passes by a town with sandy boundaries and a sandy name. Holon. At the fringe of Holon is the suburb of Jessie Cohen – named after its American donors, Max and Jessie Cohen – and at the fringe of Jessie Cohen lies a settlement of huts, the *ma'abara*, where we are dropped. We line up in the office of the Jewish Agency to receive a Primus burner with a fuel can and a spare asbestos wick, two tin plates, an aluminium saucepan, a plastic bowl, a box of provisions, a bag of fresh oranges and a long key. Dora and I follow the three-wheeled truck that contains our new furniture: two metal beds, straw mattresses, a wooden table and two chairs. We stop in front of a pale yellow hut. The door is wide open and inside a tradesman is sealing the windowpanes into their aluminium frames with odorous grey putty. We arrange our belongings – beds in the bedroom, table and chair in the lounge, kitchen gear on the stone slab beside the porcelain sink. Dora's low heels clank on the grey terrazzo tiles, the sound echoing against the asbestos panels. She says to me, 'You will see, life is going to be beautiful.'

She puts the oranges in the plastic bowl on the small

wooden table, as a centrepiece, then opens the box of provisions – flour, oil, sugar, tea, tins of peas and corned beef – and we eat a cold meal on our table.

Outside our hut, we hear the wild laughter of women who are washing their dishes squatting by the tap that sprouts from the sand at the edge of the path. They can speak French because they are from Morocco. We join them and they show us how to untwist a piece of rope to make a stringy pad, put it under water and dip it in the sand to rub the dishes clean.

After the washing-up, Dora invites the women to our place. She says to them, 'You are my first guests in my new house, in our new country.' The mood is set for a celebration, and the women are starting a party, singing and drumming on the backs of chairs. To allow more space for the tapping hands, Dora clears the table and puts the bowl of oranges on the floor. The women start dancing, wriggling their hips, and Dora joins in, copying their movements awkwardly, clapping and laughing in a way I've never seen before. The noise has drawn more people into our house, and soon there are more than a dozen women and girls surrounding Dora, clapping and cheering. They are saying words in their own Moroccan language, which I don't understand, but I can see they are poking fun at my mother, who is now singing with great pathos an old French song of yearning:

Adorable Zion, what have you done with your glory
The entire universe used to admire your splendour.

But her words are drowned in the neighbour's wild, 'Hooloohooloohoolohooloo.' They shriek like children do when playing Indians.

'Dance, dance!' say the women to Dora, and I think she is starting to understand her role in their entertainment. She is slowing her pace, scrutinising the women's faces. The party fizzles out.

When the neighbours are gone, we find the plastic bowl upturned on the floor, empty, although not a single orange has been peeled during the party. 'They have stolen our oranges,' says Dora, raising her eyebrows.

At night, she extinguishes the petrol lamp and tucks me in with the grey blanket and her winter coat.

I say to her, '*Maman,* I want to go back to our country.'

'But *this* is our country,' she says, and kisses me goodnight.

I see pink flowers with wolves' teeth blossoming in the dark wood along a country road. A group of people walking, me running in front, our mouths forming a song but not a sound is heard. A creaking metal gate reluctant on its hinges; heavy steps on white gravel. I throw a coin into the wishing well topped with crooked black wrought iron; an abyss so deep and so dark I can't make a wish. In the stone *fruitière* apples and pears lie piled on wooden shelves too high for me to reach. And walking back empty-handed I see the road split open, a deep canyon forming and the camping grounds with our tent sinking into the earth. In the morning, I don't want to let go of this image. I will repeat the dream tonight and each night thereafter, a thousand times until the day I return to Chevreuse.

The winter light lies on my face. I hear a call, in a foreign language: *Ta-pooziiiiim! ta-pooziiiiim!* I get up and look through the bare window. A huge pile of oranges on a flat wooden cart is slowly entering our street, moving toward me, stopping with a little jerk opposite our house. The fruit reflects the winter sun with smooth and shiny skin. Neighbours are rushing out with their plastic baskets. The orange man, wrapped in his winter coat, is calling *Ta-pooziiiim! Arbah-kilo-beh-lira!* I see him jump off the cart, let go of the reins, play with the scales, tip his crooked aluminium dish, the oranges bouncing into pink and blue and green plastic baskets. He grabs one-lira notes without superfluous conversation with his customers. Four kilos for one lira, plentiful, inexpensive. Greenish-orange foam dribbles onto the sand from the donkey's mouth as the man feeds his scrawny beast with a damaged fruit.

I see my mother hand him a lira and he fills her plastic dish. 'They look juicy and sweet,' she points at the fruit, looking at me, her smile bitter.

The orange man stops regularly in our sun-bathed street, putting some rhythm into our lives. Watching from the window, I see the smile fading on my mother's face when she tells him off because the donkey's flesh is raw under the leather harness, which digs in and cuts through the dusty fur.

'The poor donkey,' she says in French, 'it's a sin to treat it this way.'

The neighbour's teenage girl who had been dancing in our house now pokes her tongue at my mother and calls at her 'The Madwoman!'

The Windowpane Cow

My mother calls our neighbour The Cow and that's how I see this woman now, with horns and a tail, and overflowing with sour milk.

My mother can't help spying on her. 'The Cow is in,' she says.

'No, *maman*, I don't think so; I saw her going out with her shopping basket just a few minutes ago.'

When our neighbour is in, my mother starts cursing her enemies, pretending to address the walls but really talking to The Cow.

After stealing our oranges, they started on our tiles. One afternoon when my mother was going out, she stepped down from our street onto the sand. The first two tiles were missing from our path, which runs from the dirt road of our street up to our porch. It was not hard to spot them resting on the neighbour's side, forming two rows of three tiles to widen their path. My mother said nothing, until the next morning when she went out to hang some washing and found that another pair of tiles was missing. Seeing the two square imprints on the sand at both ends of our path and the four rows of three tiles on our neighbour's side, she gave the question-mark look to our neighbour who was standing on her porch.

'What are you looking at?' said the neighbour.

'Nothing,' my mother answered, but when she came back in, she muttered, 'The dirty cursed Cow.'

The Cow arrived at Jessie Cohen with her family at the same time as us. There is a never-ending procession of people walking in and out of her house: her bulky husband, her daughters and sons, her sisters with their husbands and children. A scrawny ancient man hidden inside a giant hooded cape and his wife, her head wrapped in a scarf tied in a knot above her forehead, her body permanently folded over at a ninety-degree angle, her face scanning the ground as if she's lost something. And there are The Cow's cousins and their families, so many of them we can't tell one from the other.

On our side, there are only my mother and I.

'Your Majesty will eat her meal in the dining-room?' asks my mother, giggling.

'But of course,' I say.

My mother tries to be happy. If she manages to light the asbestos wick on the kerosene stove at first attempt, or snatch the pot of milk off the stove before it spills, or find enough coins in her purse to buy a loaf of bread, she says with a smile, '*Voilà*. Life's beautiful.' She dips the front-door key in soapy water and blows bubbles through its large loop, cuts a radish in a flower shape to decorate my salad, or recites me a fable by La Fontaine, acting out all the characters. But I am not sure any more if life is going to be beautiful. We have to laugh and pretend that we are not at all worried about the tiles. Because right at this moment, as we are eating our lunch of fried potato chips and green salad, a malicious hand outside could be shifting two more tiles to change the pattern on their side. Soon we will have no path at all.

There is a knock on the door and we both stiffen in fright. But it's only the postwoman, standing on the sand, delivering out of her heavy leather bag a special-mail advice, marked 'America'. 'It's from my niece Marguerite,' says my mother, her face lighting up. She lets me lock the front door with the slippery-soapy key. We step down from our porch – sand, loose tiles, sand, then the dirt road that turns into bitumen and stretches away over an expanse of sand to connect us with the proper Jessie Cohen, where houses are built from concrete, as high as four floors. We walk straight to the cluster of shops that is The Centre, and into the post office. The queue advances in small steps and when we reach the counter we are given a big, heavy, dented cardboard box decorated with rows of identical stamps – 'It's President Lincoln,' says my mother with excitement. We walk back. Bitumen, gravel, sand, tiles, sand, tiles, sand. Two more tiles are missing.

Inside, on our terrazzo floor, we rip the parcel open and release the particular smell of books and faint sweet perfume, the smell of America.

We pull yards of bedspreads, curtains, doilies and all kinds of linen out of the box. The Christmas tea-towel is my favourite, printed with holly, bells, snow and lines of glitter. You can't get anything like it in here, where Christmas is a strange and even sinful word because we are all Jewish. I use the tea-towel as a tablecloth. The hut looks much better with frilly pink taffeta bedspreads covering the grey blankets, yellow voile curtains gathered at the sides with ties, and doilies on the chairs. My mother's voice is muffled, softer.

'Here,' she says, and gives me a small plastic bucket and a bar of soap to wash the stained Christmas tea-towel. We go out and hang our washing on the clothesline behind our house, without looking at the tiles. The lines of glitter shimmer in the winter sun; it's a good thing, the mild weather in this place, because the washing dries quickly.

Is the midday sun blinding our eyes? We are standing by our line, looking at our dry washing flapping in the breeze, but the Christmas tea-towel is missing. 'It must have flown in the wind,' I say, but I doubt my own words, because half of our path has already shifted to our neighbour's side and the tea-towel is nowhere to be seen. The Cow is outside, putting her sparkling-clean aluminium pots on the tiles to dry in the sun. 'Clean pots and dirty spirit,' says my mother when we are inside. Walking in and out of our place becomes more difficult by the day – sand, sand, sand, tiles, sand, tiles, sand, sand. And on the other side – tiles, clean pots and dirty spirits.

It only takes a few days for the tea-towel to reappear, this time flapping on the neighbour's clothesline with green and red holly glittering, like a flag of victory.

'*Oh, là là*, look, they have stolen our tea-towel,' says my mother. The Cow comes out. 'What ignominy!' says my mother.

'Ha?'

'You have no shame, stealing like that!'

'Madwoman, I'll gouge your eyes out if you call me a thief!' says The Cow.

'Dirty Cow,' says my mother.

They are standing on their porches, facing each other, spitting out their terrible words. The Cow with her neatly cut brown hair and straight knee-length wrinkle-free polyester skirt, beige jersey and fine gold jewellery. My mother with her hair peroxided, tinted with a brew of onion skins and gathered with bobby pins into a fashionable banana-shape, dressed in her floral dress and wearing her old opaque diamond ring she inherited from her mother. Dora is cursing in a strange language and so is The Cow. It's '*El Dio ke te mate*' against '*Tchmmzzzlll*' and I am afraid their words will catch fire. I pull Dora, tugging at her arm with all my strength, sobbing and begging, 'Please, stop it *maman*, please,' and somehow I manage to get her inside.

Not long after there is a knock on the door. 'Don't open it,' I say, but Dora won't listen.

'I have nothing to hide from,' she says. 'They are the ones who should be hiding!'

On our doorstep stands The Cow's husband, wide shoulders, square face and an abundance of grey hair. He thrusts his fist at her, his gold signet ring just short of touching her quivering lips. 'This tea-towel is *ours*, and don't you ever call my wife a thief again, do you understand?'

What can Dora do to win peace with her enemies? For her, a tea-towel is a tea-towel and a thief is a thief, and now she has been provided with another proof that the entire world is linked in a secret organisation set up especially to get her. She truly believes our neighbours are paid a monthly salary to persecute her.

'It's The Game,' she says. 'They are playing The Game, but they will never win it!'

'What's The Game?' I ask.

'You are too young, you wouldn't understand,' she replies.

She is talking to the wall, her words of anger and revenge drifting from under our thin door into the wide world; 'Death to my enemies, AMEN!'

I should be saying these words to our enemies: *In Marseille my mother chose the photographer with the white dove; she said the bird would bring peace into The Holy Land. I felt its heart throb in the hollow of my palm as I smiled to the camera. It's my smile you are stealing, not only the tea-towel and the tiles.*

But my mother has told me clearly never to address a word to our enemies. I obey her, even when she is not there to see me. She has started working at the factory that produces plastic lace doilies, and as a bonus to her salary she is given many doilies with slight faults or tears. Round, oval, square or oblong mats of soft white, pink or blue plastic, embellished with patterns of flowers in intricate lace and with scalloped plastic edges. But they can't compare with the beautiful linen tea-towel from America and my mother keeps glancing sideways at our neighbours and keeps throwing her curses against our asbestos walls.

One day, when our tiles have completely disappeared and The Cow is sweeping her wide path, my mother stands on the porch kicking the sand off her shoes and she mutters, 'It won't bring you good luck, you'll see.'

'What do you want?' asks The Cow.

'Nothing,' says my mother, although I know she wants vengeance.

'Do you want them back, your tiles?' yells The Cow. And she picks one up and throws it, shattering our windowpane. My mother renames her The Windowpane Cow, forever erasing her true name from our minds.

Jungle Congo

I watch the landscape from our window and I come to know every part of the day, every day of the week in the *ma'abara*.

Weekdays bring the orange man passing by with his scrawny donkey, the abundance of glossy fruit delivering colour into the dullness of our street; the ice seller with his exhausted horse carting long frozen blocks of pure white, their transparent edges slowly melting and leaving a trail of water in the yellow sand; the *Alte Zachen* man announcing over and over 'Tables, chairs, tattered rags, everything, *Alte Zachen*,' his cart bouncing shards of broken mirror that reflect the sun with brilliant flashes; the milkman with a pack of starving dogs lingering behind his tricycle, eager to lick drops of milk from the empty bottles with their pink tongues; the watermelon carts, with a man or two crouching between the striped green fruit, brandishing a knife, cutting a small triangular segment out of a chosen melon and arguing with a customer about the degree of redness and sweetness of the juicy flesh, presuming the customer is always wrong; the sellers of new goods in a motorised vehicle, who convince Dora to sign credit contracts for goods she can't afford, like the lolly-pink floral quilt and the long fold-up aluminium chair with gold-flecked armrests.

Saturdays of deceptive stillness often erupt with a fight between opposing mobs, Polish against Romanian, Moroccan against Iranian, Jew against Jew. What means 'sweetie' in one language could mean 'May God kill you' in another: misleading words can start a fight with the waving of gold-studded fists and the hurling of stones and curses.

As soon as a fight has started, a rumour ripples into Jessie Cohen: 'There's a fight at the *ma'abara*, a fight at the *ma'abara!*' A good fight is entertainment in the dullness of the Sabbath – no public transport, and the shops and cinema locked. Young people who have been circling The Centre aimlessly in their Saturday best – girls with puffy hairdos, sleeveless jersey tops and pedalpushers, guys with terylene trousers and oiled hair – now stop their activities and rush in droves to watch the new migrants work out their differences. The Centre empties out, leaving the vendors of falafel, corncobs or sunflower seeds with only toothless seniors to buy their merchandise. The fighters are circled by their audience, which is maybe why the brawls always wind up with threats and punching but without fatalities. The winners retreat without glory and the losers dab at their wounds behind closed doors.

Occasionally the police make it to the scene, mostly when the show has already ended – there are no telephones in the *ma'abara*, and nobody bothers to pass the word to the police station, which is a few blocks away from The Centre. The police car rolls slowly against the tide of the crowd, which is leaving at a leisurely pace and giggling at the sound of a tardy siren. By now, their interest has shifted back towards Jessie Cohen, a suburb worthy of its nickname, Jungle Congo.

The school of life

I walk every morning with a group of children to the primary school in the heart of Jessie Cohen. The classes are in Hebrew, which we are learning fast, but amongst ourselves we speak French. The Israeli-born children throw stones at us and beat us with sticks, chanting, '*Kesskee say la franssay!*'

One day Dora says she has had enough of nursing my scratches and wounds. She takes me by the hand to the ultra-orthodox school of Chabad.

'I don't think they will let hooligans beat you up in this school,' she says.

She is right, although the teachers smack the naughty children frequently. They quote a rabbinical saying: 'He who spares his whip hates his son.'

A dog and a bite

In the endless rolling slopes of calm-yellow sand-dunes, a secret city of children is emerging. Letters of the Hebrew alphabet are etched in the sand with a stick, erased by the wind and written again, ever changing into new patterns and new words. From the bottom it's sand and sky, sand and sky to the horizon, and from the top you can see our migrant settlement sleeping in the hollow, distorted by the heat that radiates off the warm dunes.

'Yesterday I saw a jackal in here and he nearly ate me, I swear my life!' says Tarnegol.

'Liar!' we call him, but we want to believe him. We have invented jackals to fill the barren landscape, to feed our fears.

Tarnegol bares his rotten teeth, curls his claws and leaps into the air. All the girls scatter, squealing with delight.

With Aleeza I tumble down the other side of the hill, rough grains of sand gathering in the crevasses of our bodies. We keep rolling down the slope until we land intertwined in the warm folds of the dunes under a black elongated shadow. The shadow moves and we halt, heart thumping against heart. I look up, petrified. There it is, a real black jackal, gazing at us from the top of the next hill, approaching. As it gets closer, the animal slowly changes into a black dog; it stops and we stand apart, looking at each other. It's a mongrel female with some collie in her, and underneath the thickness of her coat I see ribs protruding. She is panting, her pink tongue throbbing.

'Are you thirsty?' I ask her, and she wags her tail and walks up to me. Her head is in my hands; her fur sparkles with grains of sand in the Israeli sun.

'What are you going to call it?' asks Aleeza.

'Josiane!' It's my mother calling me. She is trudging down the dunes, returning from her work, now at the hairpin factory. Her bleached hair sticks to her flushed face and her scarf is sliding back, escaping from the grip of her many hairpins.

I walk away with my mother, my feet sinking into the sand with every step. I lure the dog to follow me with little smacks of my lips, *mmp-mmp-mmp*.

'Black is bad luck,' says my mother, irritated.

'She is thirsty.'

'Yes,' she says, her face softening. 'She is thirsty.'

I keep up with *mmp-mmp-mmp* and she keeps following us. We pass a group of neighbours who are preparing a big bonfire for the Lag Ba'Omer holiday celebrations, on the flat expanse where the sand meets the red earth of our settlement. The Windowpane Cow's eldest daughter is dragging a long, freshly broken branch of eucalyptus like a giant broom, sweeping the sand. She looks at us and calls to the others, 'Hey look, the madwoman has a dog. If it barks, we'll kill it; if it bites, we'll kill the madwoman,' her words echoing with the group's laughter.

My mother doesn't understand Hebrew yet and I pretend I didn't hear. But the dog is folding her tail between her hind legs all the way to our place, as if *she* understood. My mother gives her water, and bread soaked in milk. It's my first dog. I name her after the cartoon mouse. 'Mee-kay, Mee-kay', I call her and she wags her tail.

At night I go out to join the celebrations and Mickey follows me. A human effigy is propped on top of the wood and cardboard pyramid like a scarecrow.

'Who are we going to burn?' somebody is asking, and my heart skips a beat.

A man with a black moustache says, 'We will burn Hitler!'

The crowd cheers, the kerosene is poured and the enemy is torched. Under the stars, the flames are surging upwards, illuminating a large patch of sand. A small boy in a clean white shirt is playing with a smouldering plank of wood, blowing, sparking fireworks out of the red embers. From the darkness his mother appears, tall and youthful in her yellow linen dress. She darts toward her child, raging, 'Not with the fire, I *told* you *not* to play with the *fire!*' She seizes his arm and pulls it towards her; she bends over the child, her hair caressing his small limb, and now her lips are on his skin. Her mouth opens and she sinks her teeth into the child's flesh, groaning with the effort. She lets go and in the light of the flames I see a bruised red and blue imprint in the shape of her bite on the inner arm of the wailing child. The bonfire is dying. The smoke thickens; the ashes are flying. 'Come on, Mickey,' I say.

The dog wags her tail and follows me home. Through our window, I see my mother mumbling to herself under the naked light bulb and I know she is talking to the walls and muttering her curses. For a while I stand outside with my dog, looking in. The sand is pleasurable, cool under my bare feet.

Tree or Palestine

We are moving away from the wrath of The Windowpane Cow and her mob to a smaller hut, only a street away but at least not next door. It's a deal we have made with a young couple who desired a bigger place, for their future family. The young man moves our furniture, in a borrowed three-wheeled truck, from the bright yellow hut into the blue hut with narrow windows. They keep the metal letterbox that Dora had bought and affixed to the yellow hut's door. They say the letterbox is a fixture and refuse to remove it. Dora calls them thieves and they call her a madwoman.

As we are unpacking our length of fabrics, our plates and cups and cutlery, I hear children outside playing on the dirt asking each other, '*Etz o Pali?*' – tree or Palestine?

They are tossing plastic coins that have been snapped off lollypop sticks. Red, pink, blue and even silver and gold plastic coins. On one side of the coin is an *etz* – a date-laden palm tree – embossed in the plastic, and on the other side the nominal value and the word *Palestine*, shortened by the players to *Pali*.

'*Etz o Pali?*' the children are asking, and I consider which side I would choose if I were playing with them. Which one would bring me luck at every turn? Tree or Palestine?

Transfer camp

Dora wrestles with the rusty metal strips she has found rolling in the street. Using a big stone, she nails one strip to the back wall of our hut and pulls it to a wobbly stick she has hammered into the corner of our garden. From there, she pulls the strip to the small tree that faces our porch. She ties a second strip to the same tree, pulling it from there into a straight line, parallel to our concrete path, up to the dwarf mesh fence that marks the street boundary. She stands in our garden, her hands on her hips, looking at our new territory.

The *ma'abara* lingers off Jessie Cohen like a dinghy attached by rope to an ocean liner. Connected by a narrow bitumen road resting on the sand, this collection of asbestos huts in straight intersecting lines is at the end of the world, with nothing visible beyond it, nothing but sand-dunes. Apartment blocks are being built outside the *ma'abara*, with real walls and real kitchens and real bathrooms, and balconies overlooking real streets. But there is a long queue of people who want to get transferred, jumped only by those with mighty muscles, fists and voices, intimidating the Jewish Agency clerks who are usually pallid, wear glasses and speak in nice Hebrew.

I never tell Dora the true meaning of the word *ma'abara* in Hebrew – transfer camp – because I don't want to raise her hopes. The Jewish Agency clerk has told us that we aren't even a family, so there is nothing available for us. 'He said *soon*,' I lie to my mother.

I let Dora shape, plant, water and weed her garden. Most of the *ma'abara* dwellers don't bother to water the shrubs the Jewish Agency has planted in their little gardens; weeds grow in winter and then dry out in the hot winds of summer. But Dora breaks the hard soil at the side of our garden path with a kitchen fork, and fortifies it with peels and scraps of vegetable. She waters the patch daily with the remnants from our teapot and with recycled dishwater from our sink, saying 'The earth is hungry; the earth is thirsty.'

Tiny smudges of pale green are emerging from the ground.

'It must be the start of our *potager*,' says my mother. 'If it's a watermelon we will eat it cold on a hot day. If it's cucumbers, we'll slice them lengthways and sprinkle them with salt. If it's tomatoes, we'll pick them when they are fat and red. No, even better, we'll pick them green before the worms get into them and we'll put them on the windowsill to redden in the sun.'

But it is none of those. After a while a little twig pushes out, soon carrying leaves that unfold and open to absorb the sun and take on a deep-green colour, enlarging and sheltering and nourishing beneath them a bunch of tender newborn string beans.

We try to protect our beans from birds and snails and frogs, thinking they are the obvious predators. When we hear heel taps on the concrete tiles, we peer through the porch in time to see the Windowpane Cow's daughter on her way back from the shops, walking down our path to the lone bean plant. She crushes it with a twist of her heel, then crawls under the flimsy metal-strip fence and disappears around the back of our house, short-cutting her way towards her place, a street beyond. We look at the beaten plant and Dora hurries towards the corner and calls out, 'Dirty bitch! Dirty cursed bitch!'

Mata kandela

'*Mata kandela!*' Dora yells at a woman who is standing next to the manager of the soup kitchen in a shabby part of Tel-Aviv. She has just been given her last pay envelope. She had been happy to find this job after being retrenched from the hairpin factory.

'I washed the huge cauldrons, but she was never happy with the shine of the aluminium, that *mata kandela*.' Dora uses the old language of her ancestors, the Ladino she used to speak at home with her family.

'What is a *mata kandela*,' I ask Dora when we are in the street.

'A big moth that kills the light out of candles,' she replies. 'And there is one of them wherever I go.'

The death of Sammy

Dora is embroidering green, red and black polkadots onto a plain nylon curtain, in the shade of our trees. Across the street the Egyptian woman is pulling out foreign seeds and stones from a bowl of rice grains, sitting on a bed in her arid front garden. Her son arrives home with a new girl, one of the succession he brings in his car – the only car owned in our section of the street. The car may be the reason for his success with women, but it doesn't add to his credit in Dora's eyes.

'Where do you think he got the money to buy a brand-new car?' she asks, and then gives me the answer. 'It's quite obvious. He must be the one who led my brother Sammy to his death. He lured him into his car with promises to bring him over to me, but instead took him to a place where this poor brother of mine was injected with a lethal needle. And now he enjoys this car he gained from crime, cursed may he be.'

The Egyptian woman is straining over her task, squinting and bending her head over the bowl because she is short-sighted. Our street is narrow enough for me to make out the lines of pencil that trace the arches of her frowning eyebrows. Behind her, a makeshift curtain made out of an old tablecloth dangles inside her son's window, allowing him some privacy.

I have heard Dora's strange tale before, and each time I am outraged. '*Maman*, this is the most stupid story I ever heard.'

'And what would you know, you are too young!'

I am getting angry. 'You just make up the facts to suit your weird imagination!'

'*Oh, là là,* what a disgraceful daughter I have!'

'But Sammy died in France. He couldn't have possibly been in Israel.'

'And if I tell you that I saw him?'

'Where?

'In a black limousine, parked near The Centre, right here in Jessie Cohen. He was in the back seat, covering his face with a newspaper. I bet there was a hole in the paper, and that he was looking at me.'

'All right then, why didn't he come out and talk to you?'

'Because he wasn't allowed.'

'By whom?'

'By our enemies.'

'*Maman*, you have got some talent to come up with such a story.'

She pauses for a while and replies, 'I admit that I am a bit of a novelist sometimes, but this time everything I am saying is the utter truth. You ought to stop contradicting me and siding with our enemies!'

The woman who carries her fish in her purse

On a sunny wintry Saturday afternoon, Dora dips her comb in a jar full of her onion-peel brew and combs her hair into shades of auburn and yellow. She puts on her best dress. It's a sleeveless summer tubular dress with giant white flowers printed on an olive-green background, which she wears over a petticoat and under her hand-knitted white cardigan. She cleans her only pair of leather shoes with chlorinated water, eroding another layer of white pigment and unintentionally exposing the dark hide underneath. With me wearing the nylon dress she has assembled with a needle and thread, we are now nearly ready to go out towards the heart of Jessie Cohen where she will present me to her latest batch of new friends. I am proud of her, she always smells fresh and sweet with lemon cologne, and her smile is beautiful, revealing a perfect row of teeth.

But her face suddenly turns sombre. There is a last deed to be done before we leave. For this, she stands in the middle of the room looking at walls, then explains to me, 'They say that the walls have ears. Do you know what they really mean?'

'No,' I answer, because I don't understand how that could be.

'Well,' she says, 'I know for sure that my enemies have planted microphones in our walls so they can spy on me.'

She looks at the walls and gives a speech in an animated voice, waving her hands.

'My enemies may not like it, but I have got friends, many friends. And because of this, they cannot touch me. I am untouchable.'

At this we step out and walk to the main street of the *ma'abara*, then along the narrow bitumen road into the main street of Jessie Cohen, which is bordered by three-storey cement-rendered blocks of flats, cracked and patched with mildew from many winters of rain. Behind the flats a narrow asphalt path stretches away, crumbling at the edges into the ground. Rows of single-storey cubes, topped with concrete roofs and perforated with little windows and doors, sit on the dirt. In one of those – our first destination – lives the big bosomed Iraqi woman, bedridden with a mysterious illness, her greying frizzy hair dyed bright red with henna. Dora sits on one of the two wooden chairs and the woman taps her bed to signal where I should sit. I disobey, choosing to sit on the other chair, which immediately collapses underneath me. The woman points at the chair. 'Broken, broken,' she says in pidgin to accommodate my mother's small collection of Hebrew words. I rearrange the broken bits of wood into a chair and sit on the edge of her bed, inhaling the acrid odour of the sick. We watch a trail of ants carry grains of sugar from the floor into their nests. The woman says in a plaintive voice, 'I have put the sugar on the floor to please the angels, who are going to come and help me get better.'

My mother smiles a big smile to make up for her unfamiliarity with the language, and I translate for her. '*Les anges vont venir guérir la dame; elle a mis le sucre par terre pour eux.*'

'Get healthy,' my mother says. 'Live to the age of one hundred and twenty years, amen.'

We watch the ants transport the sweet gift away from the invisible angels in the silence of the afternoon.

Our next visit takes us further down the road into a block of flats, up the naked terrazzo stairwell overrun with the lingering aroma of Sabbath lunches and the sounds of the weekly football match transmitted by many radios. An old woman opens the door for us and as we enter she rushes to a low cabinet to make us welcome with stale, broken biscuits from a rusty tin. She tells Dora the same story that, no doubt, she has already told her before, about her son who got up one day and left to find a new life in faraway Australia. '*Ke le vino en esta Australia, ke le vino?*' Like Dora, this old woman is Turkish and speaks in Ladino, which I don't understand yet, and my mother translates for me: 'What has happened to him in that Australia, what has happened?' she says. 'She hasn't had a letter from her son for six months. The poor boy.'

'*Ven aki*,' she says, inviting us with her arm, and we follow her into her bedroom. She takes out of a brown wardrobe the dressing-gown that the son has sent to her. She unfolds the gown from its plastic wrapping. It is made of pink floral nylon, quilted with synthetic wadding. 'Try it on,' says the old woman to my mother, and Dora puts it on and looks at herself in the mirror, turning to the right and to the left. 'Very nice dressing-gown,' says Dora, her voice tinged with envy, since she doesn't have a dressing-gown at all. 'Very nice, warm and comfortable.'

The old woman examines my mother, approving the fit of the gown with a '*Mmm*'. '*Ke le vino en esta Australia, ke le vino,*' she moans. Back in her sitting-room, we gnaw at our biscuits until it's time to leave.

The sun is setting as we enter the *ma'abara*. We fall silent, slowing our pace to delay the return to our hut. 'I know,' says Dora. 'Let's go and visit this woman I met the other day, with her sons . . .'

We turn left, instead of right.

The Voice of Israel is spreading the seven o'clock news out of a crackling radio perched on a shelf. The boys' mother,

Dora and I stand at the entrance of the bedroom waiting for the weather report. A smell of fish hangs in the air. The announcer reads the predictable winter weather forecast: 'The night will be clear and cool.' The two boys in their striped pyjamas jump to a sitting position on their beds and cry in unison, 'Clear and cool! Clear and cool!' and the older, who is about fourteen, adds, 'See, I told you! Clear and cool!'

We leave, huddling against the cold.

'That place smelt badly of fish,' I say.

'Yes,' answers Dora. 'That woman loves her herring so much, I think she even carries a piece in her purse.'

Dora and I walk back to our hut in silence, under the crystal moon.

The false accusation

Dora inserts the needle into the chicken's hollow throat, in and out, in and out, stuffing the rice and parsley mixture inside the skin. It's our festive meal for Saturday, the chicken necks that she bought from the butcher, pretending she was buying them for her dogs.

She continues her long story about her short marriage to Ernest Lamiré. 'I was undernourished,' she says. 'It was during the war and food was rationed. I would spend hours in the streets looking for half a pound of black-market meat, and by the time Ernest was home and I had cooked it my appetite was gone.'

The cotton slips out of the needle slot. I help her thread it back.

'I made a terrible mistake.' She sighs. 'I was talking on the phone to Sammy's wife and complaining to her about the silver cutlery he had bought me. You see, I wanted a pattern of plaited silver on the handles and he had got the scalloped one; that design was out of fashion. And while I was talking like this, Ernest had entered our apartment and overheard me.' Dora rests her hands on the chicken neck for a moment. 'He had endangered his life, taking me, a Jew, during the Nazi occupation, to be his bride.'

Now that the stuffing is encased inside the skin, she pushes her double-threaded rusty needle once more into the chicken throat to secure the cotton with a loop. She says, 'One day, I will sew your wedding dress.'

There is a loud rapping on the door, unexpected at this time of the night. Dora turns the long metal key in the lock and the door is flung open. We are speechless at what we see.

In the narrow entrance stands the bulky husband of The Windowpane Cow, pushing his adolescent daughter – the one who crushed our string beans – ahead of him. On her pale face a patch of fresh blood is spreading under her nose. A group of their relatives are behind them, calling my mother names. 'Madwoman, bitch, witch!' And before Dora can utter a word to defend herself, before we understand what happened to the girl and without any explanation, the husband of The Windowpane Cow has thrust his ringed fist at her. 'That will teach you a lesson, old madwoman,' he says and pulls his daughter away.

Blood is trickling from my mother's mouth. I soak it up on my blouse and her tears run into my hair.

'*Mama mia*,' she cries, '*para kuolo me parites?*' – Mother, why did you bring me into this world?

Garlic

The Arab is walking away, announcing his goods: '*Shoom, shoom!*' He has sold some garlic to my mother. Dora's voice fills the emptiness. 'Garlic is good for you. I will toast the bread and rub some on it and you can dip it in oil, all right, my darling?'

I look out of the window. I watch the Arab walk away in measured steps beside the low cyclone fences that are only pretending to separate the houses from the street. Steep tiled roofs cover the asbestos huts, huts in yellows, blues or greens that are fading in the sun. There are ten streets arranged side by side, crossed by four streets, like a grid cut out of my geometry book and pasted on the sand-dunes. 'There is a war in here,' says Dora, 'a war,' and I wish she were wrong. I listen carefully and from behind the flimsy doors, through the open windows, I hear the whisper of foul insults against my mother and I hear my mother muttering her curses.

A plant is growing in front of our window, tall like a tree. They say it's just a weed, but for me it's a small tree with a funny name: kikayon. I repeat it in my head, *kikayon*, *kikayon*, *kikayon*, and still there is no meaning to it though I know the Hebrew language quite well by now. I have already been three years in this country and I am eleven years old. Kikayon, I can hide behind you and watch the world. In our street most of the small gardens are wilting in the hard sun, turning from neglect to weed and dust. But our garden is blossoming with red and pink geraniums, velvet-rusty marigolds, purple wandering Jew and the greens of aloe vera and papyrus. 'They are all jealous, my enemies!' says Dora when she waters early in the morning before anyone is up. She waters the kikayon too; I don't tell her it's a weed.

Through the leaves of my kikayon plant, I see our enemies passing by. Here is the strong woman who calls my mother The Madwoman, like all mean people do, although she is not really mad. I once saw the strong woman fighting with another woman. Like two gladiators they faced each other, both holding a knife in one hand and in the other hand a shield: a tin rubbish-bin lid. Her eyes ferocious, the strong woman said to her enemy: 'Listen to my name, it's Spanish. I may have some Spanish blood in me and may know how to use this knife.' Her enemy walked away and not a drop of blood was spilt.

The dogs are barking at the Arab; they know he is a stranger in our street. Through my kikayon I see him walking in the distance slow and willowy. People always walk away from us. It's Dora and me.

Dora makes an echo with her voice in our empty house, talking to the walls. She is trying to push a new asbestos wick around the head of the kerosene burner, pushing and cursing. Her fingers are black with the soot, and when she lights the wick the flame is too high; cinders float up to the black ceiling. She blames our enemies and talks to them; she knows how to, with all those microphones they have hidden inside our walls. Some enemies are invisible, living in other houses, other cities, other countries, sitting on comfortable sofas and spying on us through the microphones, Dora says.

Now passes The Comb – that is what my mother calls this woman, because she always wears a big brown comb pushed into her messy long hair, for later use. The Comb once slapped my mother's face for some reason I didn't understand.

I watch the clear square of sky through the kikayon. In the middle of our sleepy street I see a neighbour walking by with his hand armoured, a big gold ring on his fat finger, crossing paths with another neighbour dressed like him in a suit and a fedora. When they meet they stop, their right hands connect in a brief shake and then each unclenches that hand and kisses the top of their pointer finger. They nod and continue in opposite directions, fists ready to spring against my mother's face. What a funny name, kikayon, I think, and so what – maybe it is just a weed.

I hold the bag of garlic heads Dora has bought from the Arab. I open the clear plastic pouch that is like a bag of lollies. I blow and the white skins are flaking, falling on the wooden table Dora has painted red. I arrange the skins in a flower shape, white petals on the red shiny surface. The cloves are bunched tight together and I use my nails to separate them. In the corner of the bag, I find something that doesn't belong. It's a surprise, like a letter in the letterbox in the middle of the night. It's a long black strand of hair. I pull it carefully and wrap it around my finger. I get up and go to the window. I would like to tell the Arab to wait. *Is this hair from one of your daughters? It couldn't be your wife's. You are old and she must have white hair. I know! Your daughters were sitting in a circle and packing the garlic heads, and one of them lost a strand of hair. I found it. Wait. Don't go. I can give it back to you. Maybe you could take us with you so I can give it to her myself. We would sit in a circle among your daughters and sing together while we are pushing the garlic heads into the little bags. We would feel safe, away from our enemies. Would you keep us with you? I don't know any Arab songs but I could sing in Hebrew, and my mother makes up songs in French – she can be very funny.*

He is gone. I can smell the strong garlic mixing with the bitterness of charred bread. The toast is burning on the kerosene stove, blackening at the edge.

I am hungry. Dora knows I want more than bread rubbed with oil and garlic. Behind me, she is talking to the walls again. She is pleading, begging. 'We are hungry. Give us some steak with green peas. I know you are listening to me. Please, some steak and peas.'

I turn around. 'And potatoes,' I say. 'I would like some fried potatoes as well.'

'And potatoes, please . . . Fried potatoes for my child.'

Feather clouds

I spend a winter of languid contemplation with Dora. Outdoors, the road workers swarm under the winter sun. Our sandy street is being sealed with dark, heavy asphalt. The workers eat their lunches in our lush garden under the shade of our young tree, improved with a square of fabric my mother has rigged between two branches. Our grey cat Minouche brushes against the blue of their trousers, their working boots bordered by marigolds and wandering Jew. Dora sells cold drinks to them – orangeade, lemonade and grapefruit juice tinted with fluorescent colours that surpass reality.

'It's illegal to keep her at home,' they say to her, looking at me.

They eat their sandwiches of crusty white bread filled with Bulgarian cheese or salami, and voice their opinions. There is much discussion about my evasion of school.

'The jabs are against the measles, the mumps and tuberculosis,' they say. Dora shrugs. 'Poison they put into her blood, poison,' she says.

'What future will she have if she doesn't learn from books?' they say.

One of them, a wiry man with luminous white hair, gives me his giant spade and asks me to scoop the tar and spread it on the road. I can't lift the spade. 'You see how hard it is to earn your loaf of bread without an education?'

'Don't worry about her. She can draw so well, she'll be a famous artist, like Picasso – better than him; he can't even draw. She will paint the portraits of queens and kings.'

Over a month has passed since I came home one morning unexpectedly, without my school-bag. I left it in the classroom and jumped through the ground-floor window when the nurse came in with the tray of needles. In the afternoon my friend Edna brought my school-bag and a message from my teacher asking me to return to school and have my jabs. But I refused.

I spend long hours in our garden, looking at the sky. I see a white woolly bird turning into a giant feather. The feather rearranges itself into a feathery ship, passing over our roof, making our house move. But we stay here. The yellow sandy surface is now a brilliant black, hard and odorous. The workers have moved on.

One afternoon Edna comes for a visit and relays to

me the geography lesson of the day. 'Clouds are made of water and they form into wondrous shapes with names. Banner clouds, anvil clouds, feather clouds.'

'*Maman*,' I say, 'I want to go back to school.'

The coins of an old Indian

Dora has nicknamed the Indian woman The Cook, because in her house the central kitchen is meeting-place of her extended family. There The Cook prepares the food that is transported in take-away mess tins to the houses of all her siblings. The whole of that hut from front to back, floor to ceiling, is imbued with the smell of curry and stained from years of cooking, accumulated matter never touched with cleaning products. But The Cook has been living there in harmony with her husband and her daughters since they emigrated from the Indian town of Kochin. 'Their heart is pure,' Dora says. She talks to them in the English she learnt at the Berlitz language school in Paris thirty years ago. 'Thank you from the bottom of my heart,' she says.

The Cook has lent my mother an old Singer sewing machine, its curvaceous black body decorated with gold motifs, its mechanism operated with a hand-wheel. With the sewing machine she gave her remnants of floral materials. Dora sews a collection of dresses for The Cook's daughter who was named after a flower. The stitches dance, with her one hand spinning the wheel and the other hand unable to control the defiant nylon cloth. Dora takes the dresses for a fitting, which is tricky because the daughter – in her twenties – is in the habit of bursting without warning into a dance while emitting sharp yells and lifting her skirt over her head.

The Cook's youngest brother, in his late fifties, is a widower, the father of three children and a drinker of Vat 69, which never alters his merry mood or neat appearance, only the shape and colour of his nose. From time to time, he appears in a white V-neck jumper and drops in baskets of clean crumpled clothes. Dora presses the linen on her ironing board, whose off-off-white surface is marked with many burnt imprints of her iron. She flattens pure-white cotton loincloths and then folds them meticulously. 'What are they?' I ask her. 'Oh, I don't know,' she says, averting her eyes, 'some sort of traditional costume.'

In between Indian jobs, Dora scavenges for a living. She leaves our land of sand-dunes and walks to Jessie Cohen and further, toward the centre of Holon, a tidy town with avenues of blossoming poinciana trees. Here lives the generation of Israeli-born whose ancestors were pioneers at the turn of the century, the 'old migrants', some of whom arrived in the thirties, and Holocaust survivors who arrived after the war. Their children are playing Mozart on their pianos, the sounds drifting out of neat three-room apartments with shaded balconies overlooking rainbows in the sprinklers that go round and round on hot summer days, drenching the green lawns and splashing the passers-by. These people have shed their migrant skins and are now the core of this country, fluent in Hebrew, established, with steady incomes. Dora asks around and sometimes gets a cleaning job.

One day, she finds a job washing the stairs in one of those apartment blocks. She turns up in the morning, her hair covered with a scarf to soak up her sweat; the day is hot and humid. One of the tenants gives her the cleaning equipment. She cleans the grey terrazzo stairs, starting from the fourth floor and going down. First with a broom, then up again to tip the bucketful of soapy water which she pushes down with a squeegee. Then up again with a bucket of clear water to rinse the stairs in the same way. Up once more, a rag wrapped around the squeegee to mop the stair clean of any smudges. And when the job is done, she knocks on the tenant's door to return the cleaning equipment and collect her earnings. But the tenant says the money is with the House Committee, so Dora knocks on a few doors to find it, but the House Committee has dissolved, the neighbours say, and it's not even clear what has happened to the petty cash. Dora is offered a glass of cold water; her face is red from the heat.

'Come back tomorrow morning,' they tell her, 'we do want to pay you.'

She walks home, along the same route she took in the morning. There is no reason to stop at the shops when her purse is empty.

We have run out of empty bottles that can be redeemed for coins. All the same, I leave Dora with her tears and go to the grocery shop where I ask for credit for oil and bread. 'Tomorrow morning,' says the owner of the grocery shop, waving her pale arm, which is tattooed with a long line of blue digits. 'Tomorrow morning' is a common way of saying 'Never'.

I walk back home, diverting my path towards The Cook's older brother's place at the far end of the *ma'abara*. There he lives in his striped pyjamas, his head wrapped in a perpetual thick bandage, indicating a constant migraine. Dora calls him *Le Malade Imaginaire* – the Hypochondriac – after Molière's play. He emerges from his place only to pick up meals from his sister, and if he sees us he communicates his noble feeling with a graceful motion of his arm. Clearly they must have brought with them some savings from India, and by pooling money and bulk-buying food they seem to just make ends meet; there isn't a hint of luxury in their lives.

Le Malade Imaginaire's front yard is dry, and tall with weeds and thistles. I knock on his door to ask him if I could pull out the weeds. He steps out in his pyjamas. He doesn't look like he cares much about his front yard and he shakes his head in the Indian fashion that could mean no but I know he means yes. When the front yard is cleared I call him and he reappears to empty his purse into both of my hands. I go back to the grocery shop and put the money on the counter for a bottle of oil and a loaf of bread. I go to the greengrocer and get a bag of potatoes. I go back home and cut the potatoes into chips, fry them in the oil and we eat them with the bread.

הָזֶה

I was twelve years old at the time; the silent Indian man was aged in his sixties. I am slowly drifting towards that old age and he must be drifting in the sky by now.

Thank you for your coins, old Indian man, thank you from the bottom of my heart.

Monsieur Moïz

Old Monsieur Moïz claims that he is an alchemist, although the only potion I have ever seen him produce is the cologne that Dora sells in flat glass bottles: jasmine, lemon, lavender, roses and Chanel No. 5. These perfumes are pleasing to the nose; they never turn sour on the skin, nor do they evaporate too quickly.

Old Monsieur Moïz looks as fragile and translucent as his glass laboratory containers, but his face is smooth like weathered marble and his fine features set off his large almond eyes and sensuous, feminine mouth. We have to stoop down when entering his little front garden, thick and dark with the overgrowth of shrubs and bushes. The house smells of heavy sweet incense mixed with mildew and damp paper, and we have to walk sideways between alleys of piled books and bundles of letters to get to his kitchen, where he makes and keeps his perfumes.

Sometimes Monsieur Moïz turns up at our place to deliver the goods and Dora invites him to stay for dinner. The night starts in harmony – him playing a tune on his violin and advising how to cure a skin rash or a sore belly with heat or a herbal brew – but it always ends up with a major conflict between Dora and Monsieur Moïz about the ingredients she has used in cooking the meal. He accuses her of ruining his health with tomato peel or peanut oil. She calls him an ungrateful old goat. While they are arguing, I teach myself to play the national anthem on Monsieur Moïz's impaired violin; I sing along to my music:

As long as in the inner heart
A Jewish soul is clamorous
And ahead, at the edge of East
The eye is contemplating Zion . . .

Finally, Monsieur Moïz gets up and says, 'I am going home and I will need a jolly good quantity of potion to restore my health to the way it was before I ate your dinner, Dora,' and he disappears into the darkness.

Dora loses this source of income when Monsieur Moïz is transferred, against his will, to a small bed-sitter at the back of a block of flats. He no longer has space for his manufacturing plant and, it seems, no wish to socialise.

The interrupted lashing

Dense cigarette smoke is twirling in the light of the projector. The blond man has just discovered that his girlfriend's mother is black. He approaches the girl in a dark lane and the breathlessness of the spectators is palpable. He starts beating her, harder and harder, until Dora's voice erupts next to me. '*NO, PLEASE STOP! NO, DON'T BEAT HER UP . . .*' she begs the actor on the screen. Cries fly across the cinema hall in the darkness: '*Sheket!*' and 'Quiet there!' and 'By God, will you shut up, lady!'

One early morning, at the intersection of our street, an angry man is pursuing and lashing his daughter with his belt. She is screaming and her younger sister is following them, crying. Other than their noise, the street is calm. I rush at the man and stand in front of him, blocking his way. 'No! No! Please stop! Don't hit her, please!' I look him in the eyes. He stops the beating. He threads his belt back into the loops of his trousers, still looking at me, and then turns around and walks back the way he came, his two daughters trailing behind him.

Last entry

I have decided to keep a diary. Dora can't read Hebrew, so I don't need to hide it or lock it. I use an old school notebook where sometimes can be found a tiny black printed letter embedded in the coarse brown cover, an *alef* or *gimel* or *lamed* that dodged the pulping process.

My first entry is a funny story about a rooster who attacked me one morning on my way to school. Although I shielded myself with my school-bag I still got a few deep scratches on my bare legs from the rooster's claws, but I won the fight.

A few days after the rooster attack my mother lost a tooth. In the morning, when we were walking together – she to the bus station and I to school – a neighbour hurried up towards us and just at the spot where the orange cart usually stopped he blocked our way. This man can hardly be called a neighbour; he lives on the far opposite corner of our street. He is big, with a huge moustache on his flushed face and a thick gold ring on his finger. He complained about our dogs barking all night, but my mother denied it because the dogs were sleeping inside.

I saw the anger in my mother's eyes and the hatred in the man's eyes. I pulled her sleeve but she ignored me. 'Why don't you leave me alone,' she said to him.

He hit her on the mouth with his fist. She spat blood, and then she spat out a tooth. I helped her to walk back to our hut and undress and get into bed. She said to me, 'I need some pomegranate,' and to the walls she said, 'Death to my enemies.'

I am staying home with my mother. I have been giving her freshly squeezed pomegranate juice. She said this would heal her gums. In my diary I draw a pomegranate with its crown-shaped tip, but I don't think I will write anything about it. Or about my Mickey, who got rabies and died under my bed quietly without a whisper of complaint.

The silver teapot

The silver teapot comes from a faraway country and is one of its owner's last remaining valued possessions, most of the rest having been sold to provide for his family in this new land. The tea flows like a cataract down a mountain. Just before the glass is full, a hand performs a graceful movement with the spout, lifting it higher and then tilting it upwards for the finish.

The hand holding the silver teapot belongs to a neighbour, and all of the glasses of tea he has poured are for his guests, not for me and certainly not for Dora, who has never been invited to cross that threshold.

I am happy merely to follow the children inside the house and witness the charm of that long thin stream cascading into gold-rimmed glasses, the green mint leaves magnified and the white sugar specks erupting, melting into a mist of amber syrup.

It is a bitter disappointment that this neighbour has now joined the ranks of our enemies. He watches his children insult my mother and on occasion he joins in with them.

Mimoona

I tell my mother that we have to eat dairy products, because this is the custom for the festival of Shavuot.

She has made yoghurt by curdling leftovers of milk with lemon juice. I eat mine with sugar, with the tip of my spoon.

'I remember,' she says, 'as if it were yesterday, the white cheeses we fetched from our cellar in Edirne. I can still taste their creaminess.'

We hear shrieks coming from outside. I run out and Dora follows. There is The Bottle Cow, running up from her place at the other end of the street, carrying a bucket of water, chasing relatives and neighbours. She corners one of them against a fence across the road, tips her bucket and drenches him, fully clothed.

In the heat of the day the *ma'abara* is awash with water and resounding with laughter as the Moroccan people perform their ancient ritual of the Mimoona that emulates the sprinkling of holy water. This is the festival of the giving of the law from the hands of God on Mount Sinai.

I watch Dora's mouth twisting. But this time she doesn't utter a curse. She just tries to hide a smirk from me, embarrassed for delighting in the antics of her enemies.

Dog songs

There he is, the dogcatcher. My heart is beating: Bang! Bang! Bang! He is pointing a long rifle at four kittens in front of the house across the road and while he is shooting them the old Algerian woman comes out and nearly gets shot herself. She sees the bleeding kittens and throws her arms in the air; these are her cat's kittens. She mumbles in Arabic, '*Hallass, hallass* . . .' The dogcatcher laughs, and as he walks away he says to her in Hebrew, '*Gamarnu, gamrnu, al tid'agi, savta,*' but she doesn't understand Hebrew; she is a new immigrant. The mother-cat comes out and licks her kittens, sorting out which is alive and which is dead. The old Algerian woman is still yelling and mumbling in Arabic as she wraps the casualties in newspaper and throws them in the rubbish bin.

I hold my black puppy tight against my heart. I have rescued him from two boys who were trying to bury him alive in the sand. I swapped him for two ice creams, vanilla and chocolate. He twitches his ears every time we hear the sounds of shooting, which are coming from various directions in the *ma'abara*. I'd like to call him Blacky, but I don't think I'll be able to keep him. We already have three cats and our new bitch, Yooki.

I watch Yooki shaking on the old blanket. 'She is about to give birth,' my mother says.

At sunset it all goes quiet. Cheezar the Romanian dog returns from his roaming – he always comes back to our place, never to his owners. The top of his back is bleeding; a bullet has gone through, but it didn't do too much damage except for drilling two identical holes, one on each side of his back. I'd like to nurse him but he growls at me. He crawls under the bed to lick the blood off his white fur. My mother kneels on the floor and pushes a bowl of milk next to him.

Yooki is shivering harder. 'It won't be long now,' says my mother, filling a metal bucket with water from the single tap above the cracked porcelain sink. The tap is shaking and grunting from the trapped air inside the pipes. My mother boils a kettle on the kerosene burner, and tips the contents in the bucket to make the water tepid, careful not to let black soot fall from the base of the kettle. 'The poor little ones; warm water will be more comfortable,' she says to the bitch, and starts to sing to an old French tune:

You are having your little kids
It takes a lot of strain

It won't be long; you'll get some treat
And will forget your pain.

Then Dora pats the bitch and gives her water to drink while she is delivering her pups. Dora lets the bitch lick the pups out of their sacs, eat the tasty placenta and cord all the way up to their tiny translucent bellies. Then she takes the newborns one by one, except for the last one who is honey-coloured like his mother, and puts them into the bucket. They keep swimming up, struggling to survive. Dora's face is aching as she holds them down until they blow their last bubbles and the surface of the water goes quiet. My mother pats the bitch and keeps singing to her:

Yooki, Yooki, my dear dog
You are having lots of pups.
There is no room in our world;
We had better send them back.

She is the worst singer, but of course a dog wouldn't know that. Yooki twitches her ears and licks my mother's hand.

Early the next morning, I hear the milkman's call, '*Halaaaav, halaaaav*', as he pushes his tricycle that bears a tray full of milk bottles. He stops in the middle of our street. My mother walks slowly towards him and stands there, keeping her distance with her empty pot dangling in her limp hand, watching the neighbours getting their milk. He empties the bottles into the pots or bowls and then puts them back on his tray. Usually there would be an assorted pack of dogs following him, some twenty of them with their ribs showing, hurrying to lick the bottle necks; he never chased them away. But this morning there are only two dogs, which escaped the dogcatcher's gun. The milkman nearly pushes his tricycle away when my mother says, 'Can I have one more day of credit, please?'

Giving credit is not part of his business, but once again he rips the soft silver lid, tilts the bottle to let the milk rush into my mother's crooked aluminium pot. It's an act of beauty, with the sun shining through the transparent milky glass he holds in mid-air and the tinkling sounds of empty bottles shaking on the tricycle's wooden tray as the milkman pedals away.

My mother puts a few coins in my hand. 'For the bus fare,' she says.

I share my bread and my milk with Blacky, then clean his milky muzzle. I take him under my arm and walk out, bound for the lost dogs' home. The morning is silent. Yooki and Cheezar are sitting on blankets my mother has put outside for them, in the sun. He licks his wounds and she licks her honey consolation-pup.

Lupins

Dora puts the lupin beans in a clean plastic bucket. She covers them with water and lets them soak overnight. She rinses the pulses and repeats the process time after time, day after day, until the lupins are swollen and pale-yellow, and all the bitterness has gone out of them. She is then ready to go out and make a living, with the little bags of moist, nutty, salty treats.

She avoids my school, to spare me the embarrassment, goes to a schoolyard further away at the fringe of Jessie Cohen and waits for recess time. She advertises her merchandise, at first feebly and then, as the children start buying from her, she gathers confidence and raises her voice. '*Atramus, atramus, assarah grush.*'

'That's not what you call them,' corrects a young child in a uniform of sky and navy blues. 'You call them *turmus*.'

'*Turmus, turmus, assarah grush,*' calls Dora.

Hordes of children crowd around her to buy the beans. They are not expensive, only a coin – *assarah grush*.

Dora comes home with bags of small change, laughs

with glee to the sound of the coins rolling on the table. She goes to that school every day. She thanks the children, blesses them and tells them in her pidgin Hebrew that they are beautiful, clever and sweet, unintentionally addressing boys as girls and girls as boys, falling into the traps of the Hebrew language, earning the children's disrespect. Some of them snatch the bags and run away. Soon half the children join in the snatching game while the other half are trying to pay.

There is a big batch of lupin beans to be consumed, now that my mother has stopped selling them. The mailwoman keeps coming for them. She sits on a chair in Dora's garden, rests her feet and sometimes produces from her leather bag a letter or a parcel advice sent from America by my cousin Marguerite. We eat the beans, discarding the transparent husks, chewing on the nutty content.

'My enemies have been there,' Dora explains to the postwoman. 'They follow me wherever I go, they ruin my *parnasah*. The cursed enemies, *El Dio ke los mate, amen.*'

Summer wedding

The shapes of our enemies, all guests in the wedding party, are dancing on the white sheets, their shadows looming or shrinking as they approach or withdraw from the dangling light bulbs. The Windowpane Cow looks more menacing than ever; a giant projected on the cotton screen. The Windowpane Cow's young daughter, the one who crushed our green beans, is now being projected in her tight dress; she looks very pregnant one moment and slinky the next. There is the short and skinny owner of the silver teapot, who let his children insult my mother; his shadow is transfigured into a broad athlete, then shrinks to a gnome. The Bottle Cow – as Dora has called her since she smashed our soda siphon against the kerb – is swinging on the screen like a punching bag because the light bulb behind her has been knocked. The fearsome shadow of the bulky man who punched Dora because of a dog's barking merges into the shadow of The Bottle Cow, and for a brief moment they mellow into Romeo and Juliet.

The dead-end of the street has been sealed off with

white sheets stretched between wooden poles, forming an enclosure on the bitumen, a makeshift hall for the wedding celebrations, enveloping a bride, a groom, a rabbi, two families and their guests. Through the cotton walls I can see women's bare arms and men's hairy arms swinging, but I can't hear their voices, which are drowned by the forceful music of lutes, drums, tambourines and undulating men's singing, painfully moaning and monotonous to my European ears. Or maybe it has nothing to do with my ears; it may be all in my heart. This is the music of our real enemies.

I listen to the sounds that would follow me for half an hour if I tried to walk away; I have nowhere to go. I lean on the flaking windowsill and look at what I can see of the wedding party, which is wrapped in white and glowing in the dark like a giant lantern.

I hear my mother muttering behind me, her words melting in the steamy air of our room, but I don't listen. I know she will be talking about revenge. 'You will see,' she will be saying in her mix of languages. '*Vous allez voir! Vas a ver! Atem roim!*' Talking to the walls, addressing our invisible enemies. 'You can laugh now, but your day will arrive and *I* will live to see it.'

I don't turn and I don't see the usual picture of my mother sitting on the edge of the metal bed that doubles as a sofa, pulling her skirt tight against her knees to underpin her cursing, the fabric stretching, distorting the large printed flowers into one-eyed monster faces. I don't see her face shrinking in the feeble light from the wilting lampshade I have made with white paper and rusty scissors. I don't see the asbestos walls crusted with whitewash, covering up the imagined microphones that my mother is addressing.

Mosquitoes are feeding on my sweaty skin. I slap myself and I keep staring, watching the shadows singing and laughing, eating and drinking, deaf to my mother's cursing. I whisper to the familiar love-song that is being played: *Chérie, je t'aime, chérie, je t'adore* . . . The words unfurl and curl around the string instruments, yearning upward into the thick summer sky.

I think I heard, under the music, the sound of a bottle smashing against bitumen. I hear a scream. I stop humming when the band stops playing. On the white screen, I see a shadow-puppet show. I see a giant puppet beating another one with a clenched fist. I see puppets jumping all over the screen. I hear screams, and table-loads crashing to the floor. I see white sheets bulging and pushing out like the belly of an overdue bitch.

My mother is now looking out through the other window and peering at me from the exterior, like a curious neighbour. 'You see?' She says triumphant. 'It's my curse! At last my curse is working!'

I don't turn to look at her face. I kill another fat mosquito and its blood smears on my arm.

When the cotton walls are empty in the darkness and I can hear the cockroaches flying, I see a star fall from the sky and I make a wish.

Rosh Hashanah

'Was it on a Passover night when my sister Fortunée ate her last plate of rice . . .?' Dora is asking. In between her words I can hear the hum of gatherings in our neighbourhood. It's the eve of Rosh Hashanah; all traffic has stopped and everybody is at home, celebrating the holiday around the family table with apples dipped in honey, with blessings for a fruitful and sweet new year.

'I am not sure if it was Passover or *Rosh Hashanah* – New Year,' says Dora. 'But I remember it as if it were yesterday, the meal that we were eating with all the family, rice cooked with tomatoes. The rice was nice and oily – *yagli yagli* – and very delicious. Suddenly, just like that, Fortunée said she didn't feel well. She went upstairs to her room. She never came down again. It was the Spanish flu.' Dora is talking to me and to the microphones at the same time. I really think she is talking about Rosh Hashanah, not Passover, because I don't think you are supposed to eat rice with tomatoes on Passover night. That's not what I learnt at school.

'*Ah, La notche de Pesah . . . ke lo bueno . . . ke lo bueno . . .*

In our house in Edirne . . . *Ah, Ah . . .*'

If she starts in Ladino, it means she is going to go on and on.

'The preparations for Passover started well in advance.' Her face lights up as she talks. 'The house was cleaned from top to bottom until you could see your face in the floor, so shiny it was. From the outside the house looked like a huge white bride, shining in the spring sun. We ate the Passover dinner on a white linen tablecloth, laced with embroidered flowers. We read from the *Haggada*: "*Kol dichpin yete veyochal, kol dichpin yete veyiphsach, todo el ke tiene ambre entre i koma, todo el ke tiene menester, entre i paskue.*"'

The words in Ladino mean the same as in Hebrew. Anyone who is hungry, come in and eat, everyone who is in need, come in and celebrate Passover. Although I have already heard the story, I listen as Dora continues. 'Around the long table loaded with silver, precious china and fine food, my family sang the *Haggada* together with strangers dressed in shabby clothes; my mother Boulissu had invited them and she made them feel welcome, all the poor and the lonely of Edirne. *Ah*, I would like to go back to Turkey, to see my Edirne one more time.'

Now she will go on about her mother Boulissu and how she was a saint; she wore only black after the death of her children. Fortunée was the first one to go. She had dressed Dora up at Passover night with a new pale-yellow dress trimmed with lace, and had done her hair in curls and bows.

Dora will go through all of them now. '*Ah, ah*, Fortunée with the flu, only twenty-one. After Fortunée it was my brother Marco with a tumour, gone at sixteen. And in Paris it was Rebecca – I remember her beautiful blue eyes, what happened to her I don't know. And Joseph, cursed be the dirty Nazis who took him to Auschwitz. My father, with his rosy cheeks, died of some disease. And my mother, hit by a car. "Don't worry about me," she said to Sam, Esterina and me, "I don't want to be a trouble." She died not long after. The doctors took Esterina. They said it was cancer. That's what they always say! And the worst of all was the way Sammy disappeared. They said to me he died from a heart attack, but I know the whole truth: poor Sammy trusted some people here, who poisoned him and stole all his millions to buy themselves big houses and pleasure boats.'

She is now looking away from me, talking to the microphones again. 'Shame on the human race! They have taken all my family. The enemies, I curse them! We have had our share of miseries, you know. *Ya basta, ya basta*, leave me alone, may you be cursed if you don't!'

I fly away as she talks. One day I will fly away and never come back. I press my fingers under my earlobes to fold them into my ear canals, and I rub my fingers continuously to block out the noise. I don't hear her any more.

I see.

She has whitewashed the walls with lime she collected from one of the lime pits that lie dangerously open next to building sites, fenced off only by a piece of string dangling a sign: 'Danger Lime Pit', under the picture of a skull and crossbones – funny how pirates come into this. She has whitewashed the walls many times, because the lime keeps flaking off and gathering in the corners of the grey terrazzo floor that she sweeps every day. The walls are roughened with all her efforts. Once while she was applying the lime with the bald brush, a white gelatinous blob of it fell into her eye; the eye got infected and she refused to see a doctor. It never stopped weeping.

She paid a few liras to the workers who were sealing the dirt road and they ripped down the asbestos wall partitioning our two little rooms to create one long space. We like to sleep in the same room, we often chat in the dark on hot nights; the light attracts mosquitoes. She has bought an old sofa off the cart of an *Alte Zachen* dealer. She helped him carry it into the house. She has covered the sofa with a piece of red cloth and made cushions in green and yellow; these colours look good against the white walls. Above the sofa, where the wall used to be, she has made a makeshift shelf from a discarded wooden plank and she has painted it black; an evergreen plant is hanging from it. A huge green papyrus plant is towering above us. The plant is waterlogged, worms are swimming in the water, the red paint is flaking under the pot and the wood of the small cupboard on which it stands is starting to rot. On the wall hangs an unframed canvas painted in oils, which she found on the street. It's a wild landscape in bold brushstrokes of blue and green. She is blaming the world for the death of her entire family – no, I won't listen, I've heard it thousands of times before. But I will let go of my earlobes; I am going to ask her a question to make her stop talking to that wall.

'*Maman*,' ('*Ah, ah,*' she moans). '*Maman*, you remember when that man was pulling down the wall between the two rooms? How come we didn't find any wires or microphones in there?'

But she always comes up with an answer to suit herself. 'Because they are hidden in the outer wall, that's why. They are very cunning, our enemies. You will never find the microphones.'

Marriage

We keep weaving new dreams every night.

'You will meet a lovely boy one day, when you are a young lady. You will see. There must be nice clubs in Tel-Aviv where good girls can meet distinguished young men with a view to marriage.'

'Yes, *maman*. There must be.'

I have already started writing a letter in Hebrew to the introduction agency, on a page torn from my schoolbook. I translate it for Dora:

Dear Alef-Alef Introductions,
I read your advertisement in the newspaper about the millionaire who is looking for a wife. My mother is the right woman for a millionaire. She is fifty-two years old, but she looks much younger. She is kind and has good taste and appreciates good-quality food and furniture . . .

'And I am honest,' adds Dora. 'Write it, there are not many honest women like me, *va*. And tell them that you are a good and clever girl, very talented, and that one day you will be a famous artist.'

'And I will write that you are a good cook. I won't tell about all the oil you use.'

'Oh, come on, oil is what makes the food tasty,' she says. 'You will see what good dishes I can cook if I have all the ingredients. A beautiful meal for the three of us every day. We will invite him here for dinner and I am sure he will be impressed.'

'As long as you don't burn the food.'

'It's this dirty Primus with the wicks that get stuck and I can't control the flame. You will see that when I cook on a gas ring, with a knob I can use to turn the heat down, the flame will burn gently, gently.'

'We will have to fix our wobbly table. And the paint is peeling too.'

'I will put a piece of wood under the table leg, and we will get a real lace tablecloth to hide the peeling paint. Don't worry, I have got style,' she says and giggles.

'But a white tablecloth will get dirty and you will have to wash it every day. And what if it's raining – it won't dry in time for the next meal.'

'We will get a transparent plastic cover for the tablecloth and we can wipe it clean after every meal,' says my mother. 'I will cook a ragout of meat or chicken, a dish of garden vegetables and a nice plate of rice always.'

'You'd better not put salt in the food; you know how

you add too much when you are absent-minded. He wouldn't like that.'

'No, no, I will put salt and pepper shakers on the table and everyone can season their plate to their taste.'

'But the black pepper could spoil the colour of the rice. It would look all grey,' I say.

'Oh, there is a solution to that: I will put white pepper in the shaker, and that way the colour of the food won't be spoiled. There is such a thing as white pepper, you know.'

'That's a good idea,' I say. 'And I will help you with the washing-up.'

We get a letter of reply. Alef-Alef Introductions want to meet us. And one afternoon we are on the bus to Tel-Aviv, scrubbed and combed, our clothes mended and washed and ironed. Dora's hair over-peroxided and tinted with a fresh brew of tea, is twisted into a banana shape with golden pins. Her mouth is pink with the residue of a used lipstick, which she has dug out of its cylinder with her hairpin and spread on her lips with her finger.

The young matchmaker runs her Alef-Alef business from her ground-floor flat. She looks at my scruffy shoes, so I tell her that I intend to go to university when I grow up. For now, I need to use the bathroom. It's an old rusty room with a tap dripping into the bathtub, and drowning in bras, toddlers' dungarees, men's checked shirts.

We are out in the street again; we couldn't afford the introduction fees. Dora buys a drink of my choice: half-and-half fluorescent grapefruit juice and soda water, which we share – more for me, she insists, less for her. We watch the kiosk owner as he pushes the used glass upside down into a round rinsing device embedded in the counter. A gush of water flushes out the sediment of fruit; the man puts the glass back on the rack to drip dry and then aligns his elbows on the counter. Dora smiles at him with tight lips; she doesn't open her mouth any more because of her missing tooth. 'We need a man,' she says as we walk away on the wide footpath of Allenby Street, 'a man to protect us from our enemies and provide for us. A woman needs companionship, you know.'

The Angel

Dora meets The Angel in the heart of Jessie Cohen, at the Iraqi bakery where you can buy warm, supple pita bread the size of a tablecloth. Soon he is coming to visit us on his bicycle, his khaki trousers pinned at the cuffs with wooden pegs, the two short narrow strips of tape streaming from his black beret, flying in the wind. He sits down, careful not to crease the clean white shirt he has ironed and pushing the collar away from his creased neck to avoid sweat stains. He brings to my mother presents of biscuits, halvah or olives. He was named after an angel and that's what my mother calls him: The Angel. He has brought up his three children on his own. He grins as he holds my mother's hand and I grin back at him.

He proposes to Dora. We go to the rabbinate centre in Tel-Aviv. We wait in the big hall swarming with religious men; the fringes of their holy linen shawls peep from beneath the hems of their black jackets; their heads topped with black skullcaps, these men have beards and two single dangling curls which they tuck behind their ears for practicality. They question my illegal birth.

I refuse to leave the room when they ask me to, my arms crossed in defiance, my feet glued to the grey terrazzo floor. I won't let them talk behind my back; I won't let them call me a *mamzer*, a bastard. They say that Dora doesn't have the right paperwork. She curses them. 'You dirty Skullcaps' – that's what she calls the Orthodox – 'you are hindering my happiness. *El Dio ke vos mate* – may God kill you – *amen, amen.*' She yells, and I run away into the street.

The Angel loses his grin and he soon disappears from our lives.

Day of Atonement

At the time of the Selichot – the recital of prayers that takes place between Rosh Hashanah and Yom Kippur and is about gaining forgiveness from God – there is much talk in my unltra-religious school about the sacrifice ceremony. Believing that we should be forgiven too, I try to convince my mother to get a live chicken.

'A live chicken? *Mama mia, no!*'

'But *maman*, that's what I learnt at school. You keep the chicken in the house for a week until you can pretend that it is part of your family, and then you take it to the *shochet* to be sacrificed for all your sins.'

'What sins?' asks Dora. '*We* haven't sinned; our enemies have.'

But this ritual involves pretending, so how can Dora resist it, with all her superstitions and her playing of The Game with imaginary rules that she believes were created by her enemies? On our table lies the newspaper bearing what is for Dora the right date, the seventh, which is a lucky number – five is a dangerous one, the fifth never to be taken lightly – for sure she will win The Game.

'It's part of The Game,' I tell her.

We walk to the chicken shop in the old shopping square in Jessie Cohen. There, chickens are kept in metal cages stacked one on top of the other, the chickens in the bottom cage collecting in their white feathers the excrement of their neighbours above, the frightened screeches of the birds echoing on the filthy concrete path bordering the shop. This looks more like a market, with the *shochet* sitting outside on an empty wire cage, white feathers flying around him, some getting caught in his beard, his grey dustcoat caked with blood glistening in the sun, and blood running on the ground and forming its own gutter, or coagulating in buckets and feeding the many flies.

'*Bar-minan*, let's get out of here,' says Dora.

But I get my chicken. I keep her locked in the ablutions room, safe from our cats and dogs. I pat her white feathers and feed her bread softened in milk, and Dora spends much time cleaning chicken droppings. She sends embarrassed looks to the chicken, which, she believes, can sense its forthcoming execution.

It is with a heavy heart that we make our way on the eve of Yom Kippur – The Day of Atonement – with the chicken in a plastic shopping basket, back to the chicken shop in Jessie Cohen for the sacrifice ceremony.

The *shochet* holds the chicken by its feet, swings it upside-down around my head three times and tells me to repeat after him, 'This is my redemption, this is my forgiveness, this is my indemnity.' Then he holds his knife – sharpened according to the religious law – in one hand and, in the other, the bird's throat. The chicken closes its eyes in surrender to its fate, and we avert our eyes, my mother and I.

On Yom Kippur I want to fast, though Dora says that I have starved enough during the year and all my sins will be forgiven by now. But I want to stand in the women's section and inhale a lemon studded with cloves, like other girls. We stand there, Dora and I, me with a little unripe lemon, inhaling the sharp fragrance and watching our enemies and friends inside and around the synagogue. All the men and women, some with gold rings on their fingers – like the ones that broke Dora's teeth – those who mutter a curse when they see her, those who ignore her, those who are kind to her and those who barely know her – are standing now in front of the parchment Torah scroll. The men are swaying, wrapped in the black-striped linen *Talit,* their left or right arm bound in the black leather straps of the *Tefilin* – the little black leather box of holy scripture attached to their forehead like a healing device. I hear their prayer, sorrowful with hunger, rising from their hollow stomachs: '*Chatanu lefaneicha, rachem aleinu.*' We have sinned in front of you, have mercy on us.

Daughter of the sea

On the beach of Bat-Yam – meaning daughter of the sea – my mother and I spend hours of bliss away from our enemies, by the tepid water of the Mediterranean. Both of us in one-piece swimming costumes, hers of navy-blue, which she found in the flea market and trimmed at the neck and shoulder with a scrap of white material; mine faintly smelling of America, oversized, pruned of its sponge bra and stitched in to fit me, handed down from my cousin Marguerite's daughter, who baptised it on the shores of New Haven.

Between dips in the water we sit on the blue deck chairs with adjustable canopies, which we have hired from the kiosk owners, the blond, tanned Calderon brothers who speak to my mother in Ladino and treat her like a lady. On a lucky day like this one, when we have enough money for such luxury, we sit on our deck chairs as if our lives were full of promise. Dora stares at a couple playing with their baby and as she rubs some greasy cream on my back she tells me how one day I will be a bride in white with a long veil, a bunch of white roses in my hand and a magnificent husband on my arm. 'For you, I want a husband like that one.' She points at the husband. 'But just a bit taller for, although distinguished he still is too short. You certainly will grow quite tall to judge by the height of your dirty pig of a father.'

It's the heat, they say in Israel when your blood boils and your speech goes wayward. Dora is now cursing Raoul, my father, and all her enemies who, with their malevolent intentions, introduced her to him. I don't have to block my ears to deafen myself; her voice is drowned in the cacophony of the crowded beach, the many noises melting into one under the relentless sun. The sea pounds the shore, retreating with a forceful undertow while the lifeguards from the height of their wooden tower blow their whistles at the disobedient swimmers beyond the black flags pitched on the edge of the water. The guards' voices, amplified by a megaphone, warn the daredevils in vain from the dangers of the sea. Dora talks to herself, her words wafting away from me.

The air rising from the sand distorts the landscape. In the distance, a passing ship becomes in my mind a luxurious ocean liner that will take us away, my mother and me, to better shores.

'*Eskimo limon, Eskimo limon,*' calls the ice-cream seller. He trudges in the hot sand with the small insulated wooden box hanging from a strap on his shoulder, yelling till his voice is hoarse in competition with the wild waves, the children's screeches, the transistors emitting The Voice of Israel, the life guards screaming from the top of their tower like angry prophets; '*A'choutza, a'choutza* – out of the water – NOW!' Dora buys an *Eskimo limon* for me. '*Beraha i salud, kerida mia*' – Blessings and good health, my darling – she says, reverting to Ladino for the blessing, as she does for her curses.

We return to our place before sunset. The asbestos walls of our hut radiate the remnant heat of the day. My mother half-fills a twenty-litre metal vessel and hoists it onto the kerosene stove, the metal blackening with the soot. When it has boiled, she adds tap water to adjust the temperature to soothing warmth. She tips the water over me from a small plastic dish, once to drench me and then, when my body is foaming with the soap and all traces of salt and cream are gone, she pours the water many more times, to rinse and coddle me. As she splashes me, she keeps reciting the same words: '*Banyiko de novia, amen, amen. Banyiko de novia.*' Bride's bath, amen.

The Horseshoe

Dora gives the microphones an abusive lecture: 'Shame on humanity, to send a good pupil to work instead of high school. If only you had let me make a living. Shame, shame, and unforgivable!'

Then she looks at the ceiling, meaning the sky. 'Justice will be done,' she says, waving her fists.

She has tried her best. She hemmed some of the more elegant *ma'abara* women's evening dresses with needle and thread, in the home of a seamstress who told her that her stitches looked like lice. For a while she washed dishes in a restaurant at The Centre. The owner licked peanut-oil droplets off the bottle after every pouring and fired Dora because she broke too many glasses. She laundered and mended second-hand garments imported in bales from America, but the importer disappeared in a haze of gossip, leaving behind him a suburb of women dressed in semi-transparent bubble-nylon blouses, buttoned with plastic rhinestones. She minded Haïm and Yaïr, whom she called Haïmiko and Yaïrliko, until they reached kindergarten age and she parted from them with much heartache. She was a debt-collector for a frock-shop in Holon, but when she knocked on the doors of elusive customers they told her to mind her own business. She cleaned many houses and flights of stairs. But she never got long-term employment out of any of this. With every failure, she blamed her enemies.

Defeated, she prepares my breakfast early on Saturday mornings, to sustain me during my long day's work. I rise to the aroma of steak, peas and potatoes, which I devour. Then I kiss her goodbye and exit the *ma'abara* for the suburb of Ramat-Rachel, continuing into the neighbouring suburb of Ramat-Yossef and its Horseshoe Cafe.

'Bella-Bella! Wash the dishes, clean the toilets, clear the tables.' She knows I am called Bella at school. 'Bella-Bella, can you stand at the kiosk, the customers are piling up!' I sell lollypops, Napoleon cakes, Eskimo Pies and orangeades at the kiosk. 'Back to the kitchen now, Bella-Bella,' the woman calls in her mocking raspy voice while her husband cowers behind the main counter, readjusting his spectacles or wiping the stainless-steel bench tops. But at the end of my working day he gives me two of the best ice-creams, an Eskimo Pie and a cassata. 'For the road,' he says. I have to walk home, because according to the religious law there's no public transport until three stars have appeared in the sky to mark the end of the Sabbath.

For the rest of the week I go to school; this is to

complete my last year of education. I top up our income with an extra cleaning shift at The Horseshoe on Thursday evenings. One Thursday towards the end of the year, my employers' older son, who is fourteen like me, asks me when my end-of-school party will be. 'It's under way at this very moment,' I reply.

'Oh. Daddy,' he asks his father, 'can you release her now, without docking her pay?'

With my salary, Dora buys an old horseshoe for half a lira from the *Alte Zachen* cart. She nails it on our door. 'For good luck,' she says. 'Your employers called their business The Horseshoe, and look how well off they are now.'

While Nasser is waiting for Rabin

The Voice of Israel is broadcasting the army units' code names – Running Water, Shiny Arrow, Moving Sands or Tall Pine – asking their soldiers to report. We are in the month of May, in the year of 1967. The Egyptian leader, Gamal Abdul Nasser, has blocked the Tiran Straits passage to Israel; our ships are stranded on the turquoise southern waters in the port of Eilat. Everybody is busying themselves with preparations, euphoric with pre-war fever. They rush to empty the supermarket shelves, shoving each other with their elbows. They protect windows with a crisscross of sticky tape and obstruct the clear glass with black cardboard in case of a night bombing raid. The nation is digging trenches in the earth of every back or front yard, and singing in unison:

Nasser is waiting for Rabin Ai ... yay yay
Nasser is waiting for Rabin Ai ... yay yay
Let him wait there, let him stand, Ai ... yay yay
'Cos we'll turn up a hundred per cent! Ai ... yay yay

While we are digging these trenches, confident of never having to shelter in them owing to our imminent victory, a sneering youth from our neighbourhood says to my mother and me:

'I hope the first bomb falls on your house.'

'May the bomb fall on you, cursed bastard,' Dora answers.

The knife without a 'k'

You may wonder at first how my mother and I have come to associate a knife with laughter and the old Algerian man. But there is a simple explanation, linked to a mischievous moment just before our lives become filled with fear.

The Algerian man ignores those calling my mother The Madwoman, politely accepts her hard savoury *bourek* baked with too much oil and not enough leavening powder, which she hands to him in the street outside our fence. 'You can't come in,' she says to him, 'my enemies will spread bad gossip if you do, you know . . .'

This man has a gentle presence, feathery white hair, a slow gait and a soft voice made even softer because he can't pronounce the letter 'k'. Dora, of course, would never insult the lonely man, but behind his back she playfully omits the first letter of words that start with the sound *k*. Casserole becomes a word to giggle for: '*asserole*'. A knife, '*couteau*', becomes '*outeau*' in our private vocabulary. '*Donnes-moi le outeau*' she says, holding the butter and a slice of bread. This is until the day The Bully arrives. Then *couteau* becomes a grave word that can no longer go without its *k* sound.

On the day he moves in next to our small blue house The Bully jumps over the metal ribbon that separates our front yard from his. Without any superfluous introduction, waving a thick rope in his hand, he demands: 'Give me a knife to cut the cord.'

Dora, superstitious when it comes to the exchange of sharp objects between people, a notion she acquired in France, doesn't take this very well. She once returned a brooch given to her as a present, because of the pin that could prick friendship (in this case, the action lost her a friend). But a kitchen knife? Is this new neighbour playing the game? Well, she thinks, *two* can play this game. She is determined not to let him win, even with the fierce look in his devilish eyes, the sharp features, the crewcut, his small moustache. Really, he has a Hitler look, only worse because of his bulky appearance and the deep scar across his left cheek.

'We haven't got any knives,' says Dora to the man, lying without further diplomacy. The man spits on the ground and answers with a curse in his own language; and he doesn't stop all day, his swearing echoing in his empty house and travelling out of his open window into our garden and through our thin door. It sours the air, shrinks our hearts with fear. The menace is to remain, to evolve and eventually to erupt.

Seventeen days and seventeen nights

It's always the same. I am running in a dark street and they are close behind me, I can nearly feel their breath on my neck. The dreaded moment comes when I try to move but my feet are embedded in the ground; I can't go forward. I turn around and see them, the uniformed Nazis, and when they shoot I wake up startled. I am alive; in the silence I hear my mother breathing.

When I have this dream, I believe it. I've dreamt it so many times that I should be able to say it's just a dream. But the war was real. I have heard the many stories of barbed wire, swastikas, crumbs of mouldy bread, blood on snow, bars of soap foaming with human fat. I have been on school excursions to Yadvashem, where I have added my tears to those of others – children's tears saturating the stone floors under the blown-up photos of skeletons in striped pyjamas. In the summer I see the long line of indigo digits tattooed inside the pale forearms of the grocer, his wife or some of their customers. I want to know more, always more.

'Tell me about the war,' I say to Dora.

She lifts her head from her work – she is knitting tiny babies' booties in pink and white wool to supplement our income. 'The war . . . They took my brother Joseph, the cursed Nazis . . .'

Friday afternoon, it's raining and we don't have an umbrella. We stay indoors.

'Did I tell you about our escape to Rouen?'

'I am not sure . . .' (I lie, I want to hear it again.)

'I was left to look after my old mother. It was not a happy life with her, you know. She would call her four dead children every day – "Marco, Fortuné, Rebecca, where are you?" – and wore black, only black. We lived together in that apartment in Paris on rue Hamelot. At that time my mother had accepted an old aunt into our home. It was the concierge who saved us when the SS came, she stood up to them. "No, I am sure there is no Mme Behmoiras in here." You see, she loved my old mother. "I love Boulissu like good fresh bread," she used to say to me. They had something in common, these two: the concierge was a pious Catholic, always kissing the crucifix, and as for my mother, well, she would walk to the other side of Paris to find some kosher meat and then she would soak it with salt and rinse it many times until it lost any taste of beef, strictly observant of the *dinim*.

'Well, after the concierge sent off the SS she came up to tell us and soon we were on our way with our suitcase.

We were heading for Rouen. There were so many refugees on the road; we joined the tide and kept walking and sleeping in the fields at night. Food was rare and came in small portions. A bridge was bombed and destroyed after we passed it. Then we lost my old aunt in the crowd and I had to go back and find her. I borrowed a bicycle, rode against the tide of people and fell into a ditch. I found my aunt, but then I lost my mother. Eventually we found her, and together the three of us walked for seventeen days and seventeen nights, the French bombing the bridges to stop the Germans and the enemy advancing behind us. But we made it to Rouen ahead of them.'

Dora addresses the microphones. 'Wouldn't you think I have had my share of misery by now? One Hitler was enough in my life, don't you see? *El Dio ke lo mate, amen.*'

The old Moroccan man with a hole in his throat

An old couple has recently moved into the hut that is joined back-to-back to ours. Their porch is at the opposite end from our porch and therefore invisible from our place. They are very silent; we barely hear them or see the old woman, who hardly ever ventures out.

Every day the old man walks to the shops with his plastic basket to bring back groceries for his wife, fulfilling his traditional male role. When he passes by he salutes my mother and me, bringing his flat palm towards his forehead, his index finger and thumb lightly touching his face as he nods. Although he never smiles, kindness radiates from his eyes. He wears a traditional grey outfit, a black beret, a hooded top, a *serwal* reaching to the calves of his crooked legs and his feet tucked into pointy yellow leather slip-on shoes. He is short and stout. His presence makes us feel safe.

On Saturdays he takes a shortcut to his family's place across the arid land behind our hut. They own a Sabbath hotplate and he goes there to fill his silver teapot with hot water; he is very pious and wouldn't light a fire on the holy day. Then he comes back home, holding the handle of the teapot in one hand and supporting the bowl with the other, keeping the hot spout wrapped in a tea-towel to protect himself from scalding spills.

Once I saw the old man put his teapot carefully on the ground, silver on soil. He then charged, wobbling on his crooked legs, at a group of children who were throwing stones at my mother. He hissed at them like a cat and they ran away. Afterwards he came back, lifted his teapot and walked into his house without meeting my mother's grateful gaze.

It was this old man who waved his arms and hissed at The Bully when he was trying to frighten away the tradesman who was erecting our cyclone fence. He knows that The Bully will never curse or raise an arm at him; he will respect him for being an old pious man. He can talk in The Bully's language and I presume he is understood despite his condition: there is a miniature white bib attached to his neck to cover the hole in his throat. His vocal cords have been removed, he has no voice.

Independence Day

At the close of Memorial Day, when the nation has finished mourning the soldiers who gave their lives to grant us our freedom, the sirens blow to mark the start of Israel Independence Day. The alarm ascends, steadying into a continuous wail while the blue-and-white Israeli flags are raised from half-mast. When the siren has descended and faded away, music bursts from the loudspeakers and the nation switches from remembrance to celebration.

People grab their plastic hammers and stream into the hot May night. Thick crowds move along the street; families with the younger children on their fathers' shoulders, couples and groups of friends, old-aged, middle-aged, and teen-aged like me. They elbow their way inside the heavy mass, hand-in-hand and in single file like a train crossing the forest, from one entertainment platform to another, searching for the centre of the festivities. The yellow and orange plastic hammers with their springy concertina-heads make a tooting noise when banged on a solid surface. People brandish their hammers and use them to hit others on the head as a sign of affection, brotherhood and belonging. A tap and a toot for a shared fate and history.

Dora and I wander through the crowds, edging towards the main stage where the popular singers entertain us with songs on pioneering in the Galilee, love in Tel-Aviv, death in the fields of honour. We are wedged between the masses, and every time somebody hits my mother with their plastic hammer it hurts me. I try to ward them off with my looks; I spread my hands above her head to protect her from the impact. The blows keep landing; the crowd is delirious with the celebrations; the air is filled with thousands of toots, the familiar song of freedom. *'Oh, là là, masspik!'* my mother cries at her assailants, 'Enough! Leave me alone!'

But her voice is lost in the chaos. The celebration must go on and we push though the crowd hand-in-hand, absorbing the musical blows until we break away, reach the station, board bus No. 18 and leave the fireworks behind. We get off at the edge of the *ma'abara* and walk back in the dark, evading The Bully, who is drinking beer next door; we can hear the rattle of empty bottles and his voice raised against his wife. Their house is glowing, alight in the dark.

'Let's keep the light off,' my mother whispers, 'and pretend we are not here.'

Talking to the microphones

I have got stories to tell. I write letters to my favourite youth program on The Voice of Israel. I am invited to the studios to present my prose, accompanied by my favourite music. The producer asks me to participate in a discussion on studying at night high school.

I talk to the microphone: 'Well, my mother is all I have for family and she can no longer contribute to the household income, so our financial situation has deteriorated and I need to earn our living. I had ambitions. I tried night school, but it was hard. I had to get up at five-thirty to catch the six o'clock bus in order to start work at seven at the supermarket in Tel-Aviv. I arrived home in the afternoon, did some homework, then packed my bag and walked to the station in Jessie Cohen to catch the four o'clock bus to the school in Holon. My mother waited for me at the station when I returned to Jessie Cohen at nine-thirty, to walk home with me in the dark. There was homework to be done, no time to rest, and after three months I got very ill.

'I have given up high school, which is disappointing

since I wanted to go to university and learn how to change the world.'

The producer tells my story to wealthy friends who have lost a young son in the war of '67 and are keen to bury their sorrow with some worthy occupations. They invite me to their penthouse in one of the apartment towers they have built. From their balcony I see the expanse of Jerusalem, made of local stones that turn pink and gold at sunset.

A while later, the couple drive down to visit us and park their late-model Mercedes in front of my mother's garden. Dora has always been suspicious of people with luxury cars; she sees them as a negative status symbol. I invite the couple in and they sit on the edge of our wobbly wooden chairs.

I translate their words for her: 'They have a plan. They will house us in one of their apartments in Jerusalem and I will go to high school. They say that there is no future for me in this neighbourhood.'

But Dora can no doubt glimpse into the future and she doesn't like what she sees. She nudges the benefactors out of our place with her looks, her words and her silences.

After they have left, she says to the microphones, 'Now my enemies are trying to control our lives; I can see through their nice plans. They will take my child from me; they will make her an orphan. Then they will shape her mind as they wish for their politics. Listen well, my enemies, listen and back off, because you will never ever take my child from me!'

The Star

In the beginning, when I finish my eight hours of labour at the diamond factory, my mother is waiting outside on the pavement for me. Although I am already fifteen, I yield to her clean handkerchief rubbing the traces of grey diamond dust that covers my face. And I accept the coarse, ivory marzipan balls she has made with blanched almonds, bitter apricot kernels and white sugar.

Each day I sit by a metal wheel whose surface is coated with a mixture of grease and diamond powder; there are some fifty wheels spinning at the same time. Each wheel is fitted on the long bench, framed by metal beams to hold the axis in place, and flanked by a motor that propels it. The workers, seated on stools, attach the precious stones to their tools, then rub the stones against the wheels to cut them into brilliant shapes, with a nerve-jarring grinding and screeching. The workers' voices have developed a high pitch so as to carry their words over the overwhelming noise, and conversations bounce from one end of the long hall to the other.

'Who could believe that we would live to see little Gingi getting married . . .'

'He has got to have something going for him.'

'Tell us, Gingi, what is that she finds in you, ah?'

'*Ai, ai, ai*, and have you thought about your honeymoon, Gingi?'

'I can tell you what: he will climb on the wardrobe so he can dive into the bed, that's what will happen!'

I observe Gingi, who is pretending to closely inspect his half-polished diamond. I avert my eyes and grip the wooden tool that holds my stone.

I learn every step of polishing a diamond: four sides, four corners, sixteen triangles, all on the upper side, to be repeated on the lower conical side. Haïm, the factory manager, inspects with a magnifying glass between his tobacco-yellowed forefinger and thumb the stones I have polished. He nods in approval, his yellowed white mane fluttering, framed by the small grey window of the office outside which I stand on the factory floor.

One day he calls me in. He points at the empty chair next to him, left vacant by the retiring veteran clerk. 'Sit down, Kakaroola,' he says. He is handing over to me the control of the diamond drawer. From that drawer runs the traffic of stones; each stone moves six times, from one expert hand to another, from one phase to the next, accumulating fifty-seven polished surfaces. I count the stones three by three, using long tweezers, gathering them with a dainty metal scoop into tiny, multi-folded paper envelopes. Every worker has an identity number to be written on the envelope. I look at the numbers in my drawer and from zero-zero-seven to eighty-nine I see the faces of my new extended family. When I return home I tell Dora all the news: zero-zero-seven has bought a third-hand Vespa; twenty-two had his canine tooth removed; forty-two's girl is to be on television, singing in a choir of two hundred; thirty-three has told me his secret, that he will propose to his sweetheart and get married in three months; eighty-nine's son is starting his military service, and for sure he'll be a paratrooper.

The diamond-cutting factory has come close to my heart in the time I have been here, but when Dora looks at the building she only sees the shabbiness of it.

'Really,' she says, 'for a diamond factory this isn't much of a place. Could do with a layer or two of paint.'

Five stories built on the corner of Benjamin's Patrimony Street, with rows of windows, each similar but at the same time different, revealing the building's inner life. I paint the large crumbling building on a small canvas, making the utmost effort to give as much colour as possible to the dirty walls, applying layers of oil paint in rose, apricot, mauve, lavender, tangerine, jasmine and many shades in between. I offer the painting to Mr Bravermann, nonagenarian and founder of the factory, who walks in from time to time to see if he has received any mail, with a glass bottle of fresh carrot juice tucked into the pocket of his tailored jacket.

One Friday, at the end of my working week, I join Dora, who is waiting for me in the street. She asks about the man with the bottle in his pocket, who she spotted entering the building. When I tell her, she giggles and says, 'Him, a millionaire? *Oh, là là,* to me he looks like a *clochard*!

I take her to a cafeteria on Allenby Street and buy for us a sabarina, our favourite cake – spongy, soaked in rum and topped with whipped cream and a red cherry.

And so it goes, year after year.

Old soldier

I'd like to say so many things to the army recruiting officer, but I don't know where to start. I have been dreading the moment I would have to climb the stairs inside the olive-green building and now I am doing just that, with the summoning letter folded in my pocket: *Report at reception, first floor.*

It would have been a good thing to join the army, like everyone else. To wear the khaki uniform, take up the skirt's hem to create a mini after graduating from the boot-camp. To make new friends. To play tricks under canvas, sing under the stars, gossip and peel muddy potatoes, shine boots, grow up so serious. To answer the phone in the barracks overlooking Lake Tiberias or a pink sunset in the arid Negev. To watch the boys with their Uzis hanging casually off their shoulders, their square aluminium ID plates dangling on chains around their necks, dazzling with a flash of sun.

But the army is not for me, although I have been marching for years. I have fought all my wars against my mother and against my mother's enemies. At the age of sixteen, I am an old soldier. And if they say that to join the army is a duty, I will say to them, don't you tell me what my duties are, I know them all too well. Outside our hut my mother is trying to fortify our fence, to protect our territory; she is hammering nails into found plywood squares, planks and aluminium sheets. Patch after patch, she creates a bastion. The hammer's head keeps flying off the handle; she tries to fix it, using a stone to drive nails through the slot into the wooden handle. But when she uses the reconstructed tool, her blows are so forceful that the head keeps dislodging itself. She ties it back on with a rope and keeps hammering. I know how fragile that fence is against her real enemies; I have to work out strategies, be ready to act as a buffer in case of an incursion. So you can forget it; I am not joining your army. I am too old a soldier to be a recruit in one of your young platoons.

I stutter, trying to defend my case: 'I have to work to earn our bread.' But they won't listen. They say to me, 'Your mother, she can work. You haven't got a valid reason really; the army is everyone's duty.'

So I decide to show them how old my body is, worn out and quite useless. I hide in the rest-room and I swivel round and round, like I did when I was little, faster and faster until the world is spinning beyond recognition. I pinch my nose, tighten my mouth, stop my breathing and I spin and spin. I just make it into the examination room before I fall to the floor. 'I am all right, really,' I say to the doctor, sly as a fox. It looks like he is falling for it; he sends me away with a grimace and tells me to go to the town dispensary to get some help.

I ride the No. 18 bus again and when I arrive home I tell my mother, 'Don't you worry, *mdman*, I will always be here for you.'

Friendship

While I am working at The Star, Dora cleans the house, cooks our meals and cares for our blossoming garden. She gets through these tasks in haste, so she can escape the house and the *ma'abara*.

She rarely walks to the decaying centre of Jessie Cohen now, preferring the new suburb of Neot Rachel beside the *ma'abara*, with its modern shops and its tall buildings arranged around communal gardens. She lingers on the concrete benches, observes other people's normal life. She often starts a conversation, charming her listeners with light, pleasant talk.

One day Dora meets a young woman with a small son, Ari. When I return home, she announces, 'I have made a new friend and I think you are going to like her very much. She emigrated from Turkey not long ago. Her name is Jeanette.'

Jeanette is my only friend during my teenage years. She teaches me to look at my mother differently. She says to her: '*Dora, vous êtes unique.*' She invites us to her apartment and takes us on enchanted journeys with slide-shows of her travels in Europe and Africa. We visit the Tivoli Gardens in Copenhagen, a bridge in Venice, a market in Ivory Coast, while we eat open sandwiches of smoked herring and pluck chocolates out of ornate boxes, sitting on the silver velvet couches against a wall Jeanette has painted in chocolate-brown. She is going again to Africa, but she will send me photos and letters, and I know that one day she will come back.

Letter to Jeanette

Dear Jeanette,

We were devastated to hear about the death of your Ari. I cannot even find words of consolation. This is too terrible, to lose a child. I have been thinking about why people have children and it doesn't make sense to me at all. Life is so cruel and so full of danger, can't people see this? We have known only good qualities in you, but I wonder why you never thought that it is a pity to bring a child into this world. Still, we loved Ari very much and we will miss him forever.

Jeanette, we love you very much so I am forgiving you for expecting another baby again. When he is born please send us a photo. And when you come back here I will play with him or her.

P.S. We understand you were here only for a few days and it was very hard for you, so of course we are not cross that you didn't invite us to the funeral. Maman said that on Friday afternoon when I come back from work we will walk through the sand-dunes to the cemetery and put some fresh flowers on Ari's grave.

Your friend Josi

Dora reads my letter and nods in approval. Then she folds it twice, places it with her letter inside the envelope and writes Jeanette's address in capital letters. She traces and retraces bold serifs with her pen on the word AFRICA.

'What you wrote in your letter is the pure truth!' says my mother to me.

Meat instead of roses

Love didn't come into it, love came after it, when I was a baby in my mother's arms.

Now I am a girl in my mother's garden and she feeds me under the shade of the poinciana tree, with her heart and with her hands, forming little meatballs that are simmered in tomato sauce, like the *keftedes* her mother cooked for the family in their house in Edirne. In this garden, in the *ma'abara* in Jessie Cohen, I have heard many of her stories. On a warm night, my mother averts her eyes towards the marigolds, the geraniums and the wandering Jew, silvery under the moon, and I learn the wondrous secret.

On a warm Parisian evening, my father brought to my mother two bloody pieces of steak wrapped in cellophane and my mother accepted them gracefully, as if they were a bunch of roses or daisies. She fried the meat in a pan; they ate it, and then they made me. My father had disappeared from our lives by the time my body was only two protein cells pressed together in the shape of a heart, inside my mother's body.

Silent photograph

This photograph tells a lie. It was taken with the camera Marguerite sent in one of her parcels. Yes, you can see me in the picture with a plastic bowl covering my head, a giant leafy leek in one hand, a two-pronged copper fork in the other, a white nylon curtain across my shoulder for a cape, and a smile on my face. But you can't hear The Bully next door yelling foul abuse at me. You can't hear Dora, who is holding the camera. She is saying to me, '*Va*, don't listen to him don't listen. Smile, smile. You have got the right to be happy, my darling.'

The Impressionists

'Enough!' said Dora one night. 'Enough!'

The Bully had yelled at me from his hut while I was singing along with the jazz singer whose voice poured out of our small transistor. Obviously, I thought, he doesn't like jazz, and maybe he hates my voice – it was safer to shut up.

But Dora said, 'Sing, you have the right to sing if you want to. He's the one who should shut up!'

I couldn't continue my singing even if I wanted to, because she started yelling at the microphones in Ladino, French and Hebrew, cursing all her enemies to a life of crying and no more singing. The Bully was taking all her words as personal insults and yelling back curses in his own language.

Maybe all this happened for the best. I am happier now, in my bright bedroom, in our new place, painting a canvas of dappled light in an enchanted garden. I sell my canvasses to earn extra money to pay for the apartment we are renting privately in Bat-Yam. This painting is a copy of Monet's *Women in the Garden*, and my customer is number 44. I sign it 'Josi B. after Monet'.

Nearly all of the workers at the diamond factory have commissioned a painting from me. I spend all my Saturdays by the easel. My favourite artist is Rousseau: I love his image of the woman in a jungle and I am glad to have four orders for it. Each time I improve my colour matching, and Dora says my version is now better than the original – a picture in an art book.

We left our hut to be minded by a homeless scruffy young man of Turkish origins, recommended by one of Dora's friends. He is sitting in our asbestos room, making pictures with strands of straw on a piece of black velvet-covered card to earn some money. He lost his night job as a security guard after he was caught three times patting the savage guard-dogs – German shepherds and Dobermans – which was against the rules.

Our apartment is on the second floor of a modern building. There are sixteen tenants around our stairwell, four on each floor, and I follow the others' lives by their sounds. Doors opening and closing, a click of a lock or a slamming in the draught, snippets of conversations. The shuffling steps of the woman who always goes to the grocery shop in her pink slippers; the children on their way to school, hitting the metal parapet with their bags; the old man with the barking cough of a seal; the father answering every one of his toddler's questions in a childish voice; bouncing balls and the clatter of dishes; the nine p.m. news when all the nation holds its breath to hear if any soldiers have been killed along the Suez canal; car engines stopping and the drivers collecting provisions from the boot before walking to the foyer, their leather soles echoing on the expanse of bitumen.

These sounds are reassuring. I sit by my small radiator and I rarely think about our damp hut in the *ma'abara*; I am forgetting the old curses. Now I am painting Monet's portrait of a woman with a black hat. It's a commission from the woman next door, who sometimes invites us for afternoon tea.

The six months of the lease have passed swiftly; winter is over. Beach balls are bouncing again on the stairs and in the letterbox there is a letter from the landlord asking us to leave: he says he now needs the apartment for his family. Which is as well, says my mother, as there are only so many paintings I can do on my day off (Saturday is my only free day per week) and we can't keep up with the bills. A Rousseau for the gas, a Degas for the electricity, a Monet for the water and a Manet for the house committee expenses, and still there is the rent to be paid.

The young man moves out of our hut. Dora talks to the old lady across the road, who says 'Yes' in her melodious voice, 'yes, that homeless young man can live in my spare room.'

At night I look across and see the light in that spare room. The scruffy young man is still gluing strands of straw on black velvet to create landscapes of windmills and farmhouses. But I don't paint any more. There is no point, really, our dreams dry up quicker than my oil paints.

Final blow

I have been sitting by my mother's side for days now. Words keep playing in my mind, I can't get them out of my head:

Mama mia, help me.

It will take her a long time to recover from the blow. She has been lying in bed all day and all night. She has been quiet; she hasn't got any energy left to curse her enemies. She gets up to have a wash. I heat water on the kerosene burner and then help her to sit on the stool, wash her with cloth and soap, and pour the water from the pail over her body with a bowl. But the acrid smell of sickness is invading our place.

I try to escape this world as much as I can. I go through the high pile of *Jours de France* magazines that Jeanette gave us before she left for Africa. In their pages I can enter the lives of Sylvie Vartan and Johnny Hallyday, of Mireille Mathieu and of the families of Prince Rainier and the Iranian shah. It's a world of luxury mansions, sports cars, sunny resorts, lavish parties and splendid palaces. I keep flipping, and from tropical palm trees to Chamonix snow the days slip away while my mother slowly recovers.

In my terror, I never asked her how she managed to walk to the telephone booth in Livorno Street, ten minutes away, to ring me at work. I won't ask her now. It was the phone call I have been dreading since the old man with the hole in his throat moved out. When I heard her words of distress, I returned the diamonds I had been counting to their paper envelope, put it straight into the drawer, grabbed my bag and left.

When I got off the bus she was waiting for me, crying. I told her not to worry, that we would go to the police and this time they would put The Bully in jail. We walked across the sand-dunes to the police station, but we might as well have stayed home. The policeman leaned on the grey table and slowly wrote a report. He looked bored – it's true, there wasn't enough blood on my mother's face, for most of the damage was internal. He told us to go and see a doctor, but Dora was not going to surrender to a doctor, certainly not now. She didn't have the strength to walk home and I asked the policeman if he would drive us but he refused. On the street, I asked a man who was opening his car door if he would give us a lift, but he also refused. So I supported her as much as I could, and we rested on every bench along the way until we got home. The Bully didn't miss our entrance, but this time he was quiet. I told my mother not to worry; surely he would be put in jail very soon. But nothing ever happened to him; he is free to continue his idle existence and to resume cursing to his heart's content.

That's how it had started, with a curse.

My mother described to me what had happened. 'He was cursing me while I was pruning the blue flower bushes near our gate. But enough is enough, you know. I couldn't take it any more, and I told him to shut up. "What do you want of me," I asked him. "Leave me alone, you bastard." So he came out and rammed our garden gate and broke the lock. He started beating me up and I fell to the ground. A small crowd of neighbours gathered and they stood there and watched. He hit me again and again, striking the back of my neck with his stretched hand, like an axe to wood. Hard, he hit, so hard . . .

'I cried, "Enough, please, stop, *mama, mama mia*, help me," but he kept going until I couldn't move. I heard somebody say, "This is not nice, we are all Jews." That neighbour from down the street, the one with the blue eyes who is my enemy, had been watching all along and she took her time to say, "Enough now. That will do."'

Happy New Year

I explain to each delegation of workers from The Star who comes to ask me to return to work at the diamond factory that I have to stay by my mother's side and protect her. It's not easy to leave after five years of working there, but I will have to think of another way to earn an income.

As the New Year is approaching I paint greetings posters – garlands of irises, lilies and roses on long and narrow strips of card. We take a bus to Bat-Yam, Dora and I, and walk along the streets, the posters bundled under my arm. The autumn sun is harsh. I hold an umbrella to shade Dora, who leans on me, the taller one. I make my first sale, and gather confidence. In one of the shops, a young man buys my flowers and asks me out to a movie. Dora approves, but I have got my doubts.

'I only like Fellini,' I say to him. 'Do you know who he is?'

'He is an Italian,' he says, with a victorious smile, reciprocated by Dora. We have found a husband for me.

Most of my customers are affixing my posters with sticky tape to their display windows, and as we walk back along the street I can read my own ornamental writing announcing, many times, 'Happy New Year'.

Winter in Jerusalem

Ever since Dora read the weekly instalments of 'Winter in Jerusalem' in *l'Information d'Israel,* she has been dreaming of living in the capital city. She tells me she didn't quite understand the long and drawn-out story, but she kept reading, curious to see if something happened in the next chapter. The atmosphere made Jerusalem very appealing.

One day she finds in the small ads of *l'Information* a perfect position as the carer of an elderly handicapped woman. There is no salary on offer for the job, but lodgings and food are provided. We need a change, an escape from The Bully, who has started muttering his curses again, especially after my boyfriend's yellow Volkswagen Beetle leaves our place, at the end of an outing. I have been venturing further away and for longer, spending whole Saturdays with him. Dora waits for my return with patience, and the way she looks at us suggests she is aware that sooner or later her life and mine will separate.

'Keep your honour,' she says, 'because I want you to marry in white.'

Dora packs a few of her belongings in a vinyl travel bag and takes a bus to Jerusalem. I find a room in a mansion that I share with two actors, a young soldier girl, a silent cowboy from the Galilee, and Pampas, a cowboy from Argentina. The ageing bachelor who owns the mansion is keen to fill the vast house, which would be otherwise inhabited only by the ghosts of his long-lost parents, so the rent is free. I earn my living in an office, cutting and pasting pictures of foreign movies and changing the words into Hebrew for newspaper advertisements.

One Saturday I visit Dora. It's an hour's ride on the community taxi, after which I take a private taxi to the small flat in the working-class suburb of Katamon. My mother's bed is in the corner of the one-roomed flat, with its concrete floors, rain-stained curtains, and a stench of urine, rising from the blocked lavatory. Her employer walks with great difficulty, her feet are malformed, hidden in giant shapeless shoes. Dora refers to her as *La Kosha*, the lame. *La Kosha* is grumpy today, maybe because she has to feed me too.

The winter is cold in Jerusalem. Dora has made vegetable soup for us three. I swallow the soup in small spoonfuls. At the end of the day I ride the bus home on the steep serpentine road down to Tel-Aviv, wondering how long it will be before my mother takes the same route, on her way back to the *ma'abara*.

Rampage

I need to secure our *ma'abara* hut before it's reclaimed by the national housing company, so I move back into the asbestos hut. I sleep alone on the straw mattress of my old metal bed. Every night I dream about a monster pinning me to my bed and pressing his giant palm against my mouth, and I am sure I can hear my mother's voice calling, 'Josiane?' I sleep in short stretches, jolting at every murmur.

I have grown very close to my boyfriend by now. One night I ask him to stay with me. I hear a noise in my sleep, as if our door is being forced open, I reach for my lover's hug to escape the nightmare. But my lover is not by my side; he is standing in the middle of the room and trying to fend off The Bully, who is bashing him up. My boyfriend fights back hard until The Bully retreats and leaves. We dress and the menace is back in a flash. I see The Bully standing outside our window, brandishing a big kitchen knife and stabbing the metal mesh screen that my mother has installed to protect us from our enemies. I watch this scene as if I am a spectator.

For the first time ever, I talk to The Bully. I say to him, 'We are all Jews. Come on, let's make peace.'

But he ignores me and keeps stabbing the mesh screen repeatedly. I am so terrified that I don't remember escaping but I find myself in the street, the enemy chasing us away from our yellow Volkswagen with his knife. I scream, 'Help, help!' I see our new neighbour, Yossef, who lives in the other side of our hut with his young wife and small child, where the old mute man used to live. I scream, 'Yossef, save us please, Yossef!' Yossef comes out of his house barehanded, stands in front of the knife-brandishing Bully and starts up a conversation, in the middle of our street, in the middle of the night. I can hear the familiar words, 'We are all Jews', as we run for our lives, into the sands, towards the police station in Jessie Cohen. I blurt my first confession, breathing heavily, 'My darling, I love you and was so scared that you would be hurt.'

If there be justice

The judge is dismissive of this case: another neighbours' argument, he probably thinks, as he sits glum and burdened, dandruff falling on his black cloak. He looks at the page lying on his desk as if it is a pupils' roll and he reads the accumulated crimes of The Bully as you would the children's names, tapping on the paper with his ballpoint pen once for each crime. *Car theft, assault, forgery,* and some words invented by the keepers of justice, in their own language, which I don't recognise.

I have to tell my story to this room of strangers who are here to earn a salary or to be entertained. The Bully appears very comfortable in the witness box, leaning on the wooden rail with one hand. He tells the judge that he was angered by my immoral behaviour, bringing a boyfriend to my house. 'I have got small children,' he says.

'How old?' asks the judge.

The Bully marks the height of an imaginary toddler with his palm, pushing down as if he wants to stop the toddler from growing. And he adds in his defence, 'I saw her and her boyfriend naked.'

'That's because you broke into their house,' says the judge, and scores a few laughs from his audience. 'Are there any other married couples who live in your street?' he asks the accused.

'Yes,' answers The Bully.

'And have you seen them naked?'

'No,' he answers, triumphant.

'Well,' says the judge, 'you won't unless you go breaking into their houses in the middle of the night.'

The audience chuckles, while The Bully continues to lean comfortably in the witness box. He can feel as comfortable as he pleases, but I know this is his Day of Judgement and I am confident he will be punished for what he has done to us.

'Since you haven't got a lawyer, this is what you have to do,' the judge tells me, as I stand in the courtroom. The Bully is in the witness box, leaning forward, ready to sling his lies at me. 'You are going to have to ask him questions,' the judge adds.

What should I question this man who lurked, omnipresent, behind his windows throughout my adolescence, never short of an insult, his voice forceful, precipitating the blood in my arteries or cutting the circulation from my limbs, wounding me with his poisonous maledictions? I won't look at the foul mouth that yelled, 'It's about time to put a donkey's cock in her mouth,' as I walked into our garden, a woman-child back from the day's work. I won't look at those piercing eyes that are blind to the world, this savage who bashed my mother beside her blue flower bushes.

The judge says to me, 'Are you going to talk? The court is waiting.'

Yes, I would talk if I could. I'd like to tell the judge, *Your Honour, what do you know about suffering or about justice? Mr Judge, a ray of sun is entering through the upper window of the courtroom; I can see the dust dancing. Hey, Judge, now can I go out and play?*

The judge tells off the accused for victimising his neighbours, orders him to mind his own business next time and dismisses him with a warning. The Bully is free. I wait for a while before I go out, so that I don't have to see him.

There is something I learned at my religious school and I remember it now.

If there be justice, let it show up now, and if not, forever be it damned.

The last word

Dora can't bear living with *La Kosha* any more. I go to Jerusalem to keep her company on the journey back to the *ma'abara*. She unpacks a bag of groceries on the train: biscuits, fruits and nuts. 'Eat,' she says. 'Eat up to get back the strength that life is sucking out of you.' I have told her about our night of horror, taking care to explain that my boyfriend was there only to protect me and he certainly didn't touch me.

'Swear to me that this is true,' she says.

'I swear. He is very respectful of me.'

She is moved when we find him waiting for us on the platform at the station in Tel-Aviv, running towards us to take her bags. He drives us back to the *ma'abara*.

When he is gone, she starts yelling inside our hut: 'We'll see who has the last word! You and all my enemies will pay dearly for this injustice! *El Dio ke vos mate, amen!*'

I try to calm her down. She looks at me, her face twisted with pain. 'You see, I told you that this bastard was being paid by my enemies. They want us dead. But they will die first, I assure you. And cursed will be this country if justice isn't done!'

The Bully doesn't reply.

My boyfriend says nothing when I tell him about the trial. He keeps coming to our place; he takes me to the movies.

And The Bully keeps quiet.

Sunflower seeds and peanuts

Our neighbours move out and soon their dwelling is amputated from our twin-hut. The flimsy inner dividing-wall is exposed to the elements. Dora is waving her arms, protesting.

'Don't worry lady, it will be all right,' says one of the workers, asbestos dust on his bushy eyebrows. The workers patch up the wall with planks recycled from the wrecking, then move to the other corner of the *ma'abara* and swing their hammer at another hut. Scraps of shattered asbestos, timber and terrazzo tiles that didn't make it to the rubbish tip accumulate around the remaining widowed, semi-detached huts, and over time the *ma'abara* comes to resemble a war-torn zone. In the end, it will be flattened and its inhabitants scattered into the many new sprawling suburbs of apartments. The only record of this place will be in people's memories. I'd like to forget the *ma'abara*, but I need something good to remember from my Israeli childhood.

There is a lot to be said about the seller of sunflower seeds and peanuts. Even if I can't recall him ever smiling to another person, and despite the fact that there was nothing appealing about his appearance or personality, I will always be able to picture him clearly.

He was tall and well built, slowing down as people tend to do on reaching their sixth decade. His complexion was of a dark olive, his nose not unlike a potato, his round face all the more clownish because of his perpetually serious expression. He always wore an old, dull three-piece suit and a faded fedora. He spoke Ladino with my mother, but he was stingy with his words. His wife always spoke more than him, especially while she made spinach-and-cheese *boreks* with her sisters and daughters every Friday morning. I listened to their conversations and learnt a new language. I remember his wife's name – Djoya, which means jewel – but I have forgotten his name, or maybe I never knew it. Dora had nicknamed him *Le Garanimeur*.

On Saturdays most people busied themselves eating various seeds and nuts, sunflower seeds mostly. They invested much labour in drawing out the grain, biting the tip and cracking open the shell, extracting the nutty seed with teeth and tongues, spitting the husk and chewing its contents, then starting the cycle again while flicking the empty grey-and-white shells off their skirts or trousers. They mostly ate sitting outdoors, watching the world go by.

But *Le Garanimeur* . . . He sold his merchandise out of a small rectangular glass basket trimmed with lead, and divided into two compartments, each with a hinged glass lid – one for peanuts and one for sunflower seeds. He dispensed these in tiny paper bags, bag after bag, which he filled with a measuring scoop and then added a few extra seeds or nuts as a bonus. Yet the level inside the glass basket never seemed to recede. He announced his wares with a melancholic, repetitive tune, his voice ascending and descending:

'*Gar-ee-neem / bot-neem / gar-ee-neem / bot-neem.*'
Seeds / peanuts / seeds / peanuts.

He was always courteous to us, conducting his commerce with the blessing '*Todo bueno*' – all the best. His voice was gracious, no matter who was his customer. He was seated at the same corner every day of the year, every year of my childhood in Israel. He was my point of reference.

Separation

Bride's bath

Dora is sitting among her potted plants, gazing at the empty paddock that stretches away from our balcony.

'I am glad that you are intact and can marry in white,' she says, unsuspecting that my future husband has already paid in cash for the abortion I had before we decided to get married. 'If this man had dared to disgrace you before the marriage, God would have killed him,' she adds, her needle pricking and stitching fabric roses into a white piece of tulle, my bridal veil.

After fourteen years in the *ma'abara*, we have been granted by the national housing company Amidar – an arrangement of the words 'my people' and 'dwell' – one of its flats on Degania Street in the township of Holon. It's a small flat, in a two-storey building with thin, weathered walls, and fake-terracotta roof tiles once red but now faded to a shade of maroon. The interior is old and rudimentary, unlike the new apartment we rented in Bat-Yam a few years ago. But Dora is grateful to be out of the *ma'abara*. Every day she scrubs the floors and washes the windows. She then goes on walks around the neighbourhood, scanning the gardens and asking for cuttings, potting and watering to garnish our small balcony.

'Finally,' she says, 'a place of rest for my old days, and it's not too early!'

She is sixty-two years old and I am twenty-three.

We should be happy, now that she has started getting the old-age allowance and I don't need to earn money in order to put food on our table. But our separation is looming. I am about to get married.

I try on the veil in front of the bathroom mirror, pinning it into my curls. I look ridiculous disguised as a bride. Dora wanted to sew my dress, but I refused to let her stitch all her desires into yards of satin, lace and tulle.

On my wedding morning I drape my borrowed white Indian cotton dress over the back of a chair. Dora hands me the veil. But I have decided I won't have it, no, no, no! She yells, 'What an ungrateful, disgraceful daughter!'

I storm out to go to the *mikvah* for my obligatory 'bride's bath'. We have a bathtub in our new place, but according to rabbinical law this ritual must take place in the *mikvah*. I cry on the bus, and when I enter the old public baths I'd like to set fire to the building. A woman with black fingernails, wearing a flowerpot hat to cover her head in the religious fashion, writes my name on a form and sends me to 'get washed'. I stand under a rusty shower in a cubicle lined with chipped, mouldy, yellowing tiles. The water spurts in alternate bursts of scalding and icy-cold water; I squeeze against the cold tiles and my bladder shrinks.

I put on the greying-white cotton gown the woman hands me, and I descend the slippery steps into a deep pool. The woman yells instructions at me, her voice echoing between the expanse of ceramic tiles and water, overcoming the noise of ablutions. I submerge my head three times in the water as I have been told to do. Urine is leaking from my suppressed bladder, dissolving into the holy waters. My lips are trembling as I repeat the ritual lines of prayer.

'What happened, sweetie. It's bad luck to cry on your wedding day,' she yells.

I can't yell back about all the years my mother has recited. '*Banyiko de novia*' as she poured warm water over my body. Bride's bath. Amen, amen.

'I will wear the veil my mother has made for me,' I whisper as I step out of the water.

Barren bride

Once I was a baby, not quite born yet, with cold air on my head while my body was still engaged inside my mother's. I slid out onto the moist hospital sheet, wondering if I would bleed to death when my umbilical cord was cut. I survived and lived for the next twenty-three years attached to my mother by threads of love and pain.

Now I have severed those threads to unite with a man, my ovaries fecund and expected to yield. But I refuse: I don't want to squeeze out of my body a baby covered in blood, to sever its umbilical cord, to push another human into this confusion of soulless bodies and wounded souls. I have seen the world the way it really is, beyond the dubious love involved in the act of conception.

Over the years, I heard Dora repeat a statement she had heard in France: '*La moitié du monde emmerde l'autre moitié.*' If half of the world gives the other half the shits, what is the point of continuing to populate it? This could be the reason Dora never asks me about children. My husband – who has married me under the *houpah* of embroidered blue velvet, with a blessing from the rabbi for many healthy children – doesn't dare mention it; the word child is taboo in our house.

One day his mother comes for a visit, to utter the unspeakable. She sits on the edge of the rococo armchair we have upholstered with striped velvet, even though I would have preferred denim. She holds on to her brown vinyl handbag, her earnest olive face framed with her short white hair, her voice pleading as she addresses me.

'What else have you got to do in your life? Soon you will get bored. You put the baby in a pusher and take him shopping with you. When he is sick you take him to the doctor; you get to chat with all the other mothers in the waiting-room. Children give you a life.'

She leaves defeated.

Strange world

In the picture-framing shop we have opened on Ben-Yehuda Street in Tel-Aviv, we explore shapes beyond the square. We crown oblong wooden frames with triangles and arches in Byzantine style, shapes much appreciated by our customers. For a while we work together, sharing sandwiches in the park during the mandatory closure between one and four in the afternoon.

At the end of the year I break away and enrol in a film-making course. At first I shoot photogenic objects with a silent 8-mm camera. I spend much time at the rubbish tip, romanticising the life of the guard who has built himself a shanty out of odd planks and two new but tainted fridge doors, and decorated it with imperfect plastic flowers. But when I move on to a 16-mm camera with a sound recorder, I am uneasy with words. Not only do I not know the answers to life's problems, I don't even know the questions.

I have observed my mother grow older alongside me and I have recorded our life in a long accumulation of pictures that I can replay in my mind. Dora washing our clothes in the toilets of the Montpellier railway station, to keep us vagrants clean; Dora charging towards me in the Jardins du Luxembourg to grab my hand when an unsuspecting woman is about to walk between us; Dora hand-feeding a cat dying of rabies; Dora pretending to play on Monsieur Moïz's impaired violin, just for the photo. In the early days of my childhood I would say things like '*Maman*, don't worry' or 'Stop crying' or 'Stop cursing', but what could I say to her when her mouth was bleeding after she has been punched by one of our enemies? Only a hug, the cleaning of her wound with a moist shred of fabric, and the squeezing of pomegranate juice to heal her gums could express my sorrow and my love. What was I to make out of *our* world, Dora's and mine? I had learned to separate *her* world from the real world, but what am I to make out of *my* world?

After two years of film-making studies I realise I should have chosen still photography. My universe is merely an assortment of fragments, and I don't want to comment with complete phrases on what I cannot fathom. I am standing by a cameraman who is shooting reels of film. I invent questions to ask the interviewees, nodding at their answers. I find my own voice weak and I edit it out of the story. I feel like an impostor, representing Israeli television while I don't even know who I am or how I am supposed to walk among my fellow humans.

Good sugar

In between sporadic film assignments, I immerse myself in house renovations. We have bought an old apartment in Jaffa, in a small street that descends to a rock face overhanging a beach. We often walk the few steps towards the cliff's edge and sit in the house of our neighbours Ziva and Yoram, listening to the surf and eating the hot jam donuts or crunchy bagels we get at midnight from the corner bakery.

Dora rings me at five o'clock in the morning to ask if I have some empty jam jars for her. I am angry with her about this violation of our sleep.

'*Oh, là là,* how difficult you are! Rise early, and be early to bed, if you want to stay healthy.'

'Well, I don't!' I answer, and hang up.

In the afternoon Dora leaves her flat on Degania Street to visit me with jars of home-made strawberry jam. She asks for the empty ones, but they are still full.

'Why don't you eat it?' she says, 'I make this jam with *good* sugar,' meaning that she has hidden the sugar jar under her bed in case her neighbours have any intention of poisoning it when she is out. If she suspects her cooking oil has been touched she reserves it for external use. When I go to her place for our regular Friday dinner, my version of Monet's *Women in the Garden* is shining, smelling of peanut oil. While my husband is in Bat-Yam, sitting at his mother's large table, eating the dinner she has cooked for him and her other children and grandchildren, I am sitting in Holon with Dora, by the small wooden table, eating her dish of chicken smothered with the sour sauce *agristada*.

While I eat her food she looks at me, scrutinising my face and pouring out her words of counsel. 'Eat two hard-boiled eggs every morning, beware of those who call themselves friends, and never, never wear anything black, the colour of mourning. You know how my enemies want me dead, there is no need to support their plans.'

After the round of advice she inevitably moves on to her central theme, the story of her brother Sammy, which occupies a larger and larger portion of her thoughts. She curses the thieves she believes stole Sammy's money, and all her enemies, her words streaming out and fusing into a monotone drool while I drift into sleep on her sofa.

'Wake up, my daughter,' she says. 'I am lonely.'

I want to tell her that I am lonely too, despite my husband's devotion to me – or maybe because of it – but I say nothing. My mother reads my thoughts.

'My daughter, are you happy? Tell me the truth,' she asks.

'Yes,' I lie.

'Watch out and keep an eye on yourself. Husbands are in the dirty habit of slowly poisoning their wives.'

While my mother conjures her unconventional theories, I explore for five years in that apartment all the corners of my married life. The love, the passion, the new blue tiles in the kitchen and the blue horizon from our balcony facing the Mediterranean. In the winter the sea raises a storm to smash the terracotta pots, flake the whitewash off the walls, shake the windowpanes, blow the balcony door open, and cool down our soup.

'Close that door!' I yell to my startled husband, tears in my eyes.

The other side of the world

I am free but at the same time crushed by loneliness, now that my husband has left. I look out at the Mediterranean, onto the endless stretch of water. Every morning when I step out onto the balcony, rubbing sleep from my eyes, I see a new version of the sea, unique and unrepeatable. The reef across from my place – a flat Lilliputian island – changes with the seasons, sometimes bright green with algae and then white when the algae dries, sometimes submerged by the tide but outlined with brown rocks. Sometimes there are surprise visitors, like a flock of white migrating birds, or a fisherman dark in his bright-yellow raincoat and enveloped with the mist of dawn. One morning I see, sailing past my reef, a wooden boat like the pirate ships in movies, painted in bright colours. My eyes are still veiled with sleep, and before I can identify it the boat has slipped away. I am left stranded on my balcony, possessed by a yearning to travel to the other side of the world.

In a travel shop I buy a big backpack with a hippopotamus label stitched on its outer pocket. I copy from the travellers' notes long passages about Israeli-friendly hostels in Thailand, Burma and Nepal. I find American tenants who are happy to pay in advance with US dollars for a one-year lease on my apartment.

On my Friday afternoon visit to Dora's place, we sit on her balcony overlooking the sandy paddock dotted with thistle, hardy, grey bushes and rusty car skeletons. This landscape never changes.

I tell Dora that I am going to the Far East.

'What is there in the Far East that you are looking for?' she asks, her face darkening.

In Kathmandu I walk at midnight to the post office at the edge of town to call my mother.

'*Allô, ma chérie,* you are in Nepal?' She repeats the word Nepal and giggles. 'Oh, in Nepal! And how long will you stay there?'

I walk along the roads. At the doorway of a house I see a mother pulling nits out of her daughter's long black hair. When I was a child in the *ma'abara* Dora used to immerse my hair at night in a mixture she prepared, with equal parts of petrol, vinegar and cooking oil. In the morning she raked out the dead lice with a lice-comb. I buy an ornamented wooden lice-comb that I will show her when I go back. I light candles in a temple, enjoy the beauty of the Buddha gleaming with hundreds of lights.

But I don't want to engage in a new religion, I just want to keep on moving, get to the other side of the world. I keep carrying my backpack, filling it up with souvenirs of cloth, silver, glass or wood. I don't know what I am searching for and therefore I don't know if I have found it yet. I send postcards to Dora every week, telling her I am happy, words written in haste on the back of beautiful landscapes I have explored.

In Bangkok I visit the house of Jim Thompson, the king of silk. This mansion of dark teak walls has been left intact since the day its owner disappeared in Malaysia. The sofas are adorned with rows of silk-covered cushions: fuchsia, turmeric, lime, aqua, emerald cherry, saffron. I imagine Dora's cushions in green, red and yellow aligned on the old sofa on a Friday night, a testimony to my absence.

I buy a train ticket to the island of Ko Samui, but two hours before departure time, without a valid reason, I redeem my ticket and take a bus to the island of Phuket. On the sleepy beach of Nai Harn, I feel I have reached my El Dorado. I have been pining for it all my life. The limpid aqua sea and the white sand, the coconut palms and the honey dripping from tropical fruit are as far away as I can get from my painful memories. I'd like to stay in this paradise for ever.

But this place is a tourist paradise. I learn in time that the traveller here is given only a limited lease. One tourist must make room for the next one, each moving on with an assortment of souvenirs.

By the night sea shimmering with plankton I meet a man. I follow him along the shore and he follows me into my bungalow. After an impromptu honeymoon – which will have to suffice for the forthcoming long years of hardship – I follow him to Australia.

'*Allô*, where are you, *ma chérie*? In Australia? Are you telling me the truth? You sound as if you are at home.' Dora's voice is shaky.

It's a cold January, in Melbourne, not the summer I expected. I haven't got a coat; I huddle against my man, who wants to marry me. I need to pick up the life I left in Israel and bring it to conclusion, so we can start anew.

Sour sauce

We visit Dora on Degania Street. She talks to this tall stranger in her basic English. 'I love my daughter from the bottom of my heart,' she says to him.

'So do I,' he says to her.

'Quelle est la différence, d'un homme à l'autre? Ils sont tous les mêmes!' she says. She has always told me that all men are the same – protectors and destroyers, givers of respect and disrepute, chameleons who need to be closely watched. And Australia is so far away.

While I wander with a film crew in the Galilee or edit my stories in Jerusalem, my man is spending the summer on the beaches of Tel-Aviv. The Mediterranean is soiled with oil leaks and the sand along its shores is dotted with blobs of tar that cling to the skin. At the beach's exit he scrubs his soles at one of the cleaning tubs, which are filled with kerosene and equipped with coarse brushes for this purpose. He dreams of the ocean. Six months in Israel and he still doesn't know how to force his way into a bus through a crowd of impatient commuters. The drivers close the concertina doors on the bodies of slow passengers, and he is left alone on the footpath, not knowing how to express his anger in Hebrew. 'Push!' I say to him, and he looks at me as if I've said 'Kill!'

At night we reunite in the overpriced ground-floor, two-room flat we have rented. All my friends live in homes bought by their parents. This town of white houses and lush vegetation will eject me, the penniless. Of the two of us, I know I will be the emigrant.

We visit Dora every Friday night. I tell her stories about Australia, where exotic birds fly in public parks and people seem to mind their own business, saying sorry when it is *you* who have accidentally stepped on their toes. 'You would be happy there,' I say, and she nods.

Now that she has a real stove and enough ingredients, she makes up recipes from her childhood memories. Out of her small kitchen come dishes of plums with garlic, zucchini peels in lemon juice, zucchini flesh with tomatoes and rice flooded in peanut oil, and chicken pieces covered in a warm silky blanket of *agristada*, sharp with lemon and creamy with eggs, flour and oil. We eat our food in silence; our departure time is nearing.

הֹוֶה

I have never made *agristada* for my daughter. The memory of that flavour is too painful.

The blue cat

The tale of my separation from my mother is written on the back of a blue cat. I bought this postcard in Paris, thinking I would copy it onto a big canvas to decorate her new home in Australia. She would have liked it. A big and fluffy cat sits on a velvet patch of grass under a blue sky with ornamental clouds, surrounded by lily-of-the-valley and with three little birds pecking at some seeds in front of his paws, the blue mane arranged symmetrically around his bulbous muzzle and giant yellow eyes. Standing in an airport post office on my way to Melbourne, I wrote a few lines on the back of the postcard, before slipping it into an envelope: *Here's a cat that will wait quietly in your drawer for the day you bring it to Australia.*

Two years later, after many difficult phone conversations, I receive the postcard in Australia. She has sent it back to me in an envelope, scribbled with her writing in the blank space reserved for the address, side by side with my first message:

I am very sad to think that you deprecate me, for they have made a blind person out of me and as well they have riddled me with needles, which have made me look ugly and old. But today I am better than before, everybody here says so. I am now the most sane and strong. Since your birth, in every way, they have tried to separate you from me.

Yet it was not her enemies who separated us. I am the one who boarded a plane to follow my man to this new country, leaving her behind with a stack of sponsorship forms. But she refused to agree to a medical check-up: stubborn, she folded up the sponsorship papers and most likely put them in that cupboard under the rotting wood saturated by overflowing pots of wandering Jew. I know the plant will be growing fast and Dora will be hammering a nail into the walls of her flat on Degania Street, to guide the plant on strings across the room.

'Did you go to the embassy?' I asked her many times on the phone.

'No,' she replied, 'it was raining today.' That was in the Holon winter, when I told her I was pregnant.

Another time she said 'It was too hot.' This was in her summer, after my baby was born – the baby I had at the age of thirty-four, fearing the ticking of my biological clock. When I insisted, she said, 'Of course I want to come to Australia and be with you. But the doctors, you know, I don't trust them at all . . . They got my family – Marco, Fortunée, Rebecca, Esterina . . .'

One day I despaired. I sobbed and yelled, 'Please, please-go-to-the-em-ba-ssy!' until I lost my voice.

'*Oh, là là,* you are too nervous, you must be drinking too much coffee,' she said.

She always drank a lot of coffee herself, believing it was the antidote to the poison we were all administered by the evil forces in our daily lives. When she rang me and complained about her neighbour's attempts to poison her food while she was out, I could smell coffee wafting on her breath through the telephone mouthpiece – the bitter scent of forthcoming trouble.

I nurse my baby. 'My dear girl,' I whisper as I look at her tiny face, 'forgive your grandmother for not coming here to see you, for she is mad.'

Veiled eyes

Dora is turning blind. Her good eye is veiled with a cataract and still she doesn't want to see a doctor, resisting my friends' attempts to get her to a specialist. She was taken by surprise with her sudden loss of sight and has lost her bearings too, unable to find her way to the shops and buy her groceries.

She won't open her door for my friend Ziva, who leaves a box of food at her doorstep. Later, Dora eats a few mouthfuls, tentative and suspicious. When Ziva returns with more food and calls her name, Dora greets her from her balcony with a tirade of insults, believing her belly is aching with poison.

Ziva warns me on the phone that unless I come to Israel and take her to the hospital, my mother will die of starvation. But who is going to look after her when I leave again? We decide to bring Dora to Australia on a tourist visa and hope she will be allowed to stay here on compassionate grounds.

I ring our long-time friend Jeanette and ask her to help with the passport. Dora is happy enough to go with

Jeanette for a car ride, but when they get to the photographer's shop she refuses to sit in front of the camera, deaf to Jeanette's pleadings. She gives me her simple explanation on the phone. 'I won't let anybody take my picture while I am blind. *Oh, non alors!* My blindness would be eternalised and that's my enemies' wish! I won't let them win!'

I have to go to Israel with my baby; it is my duty and my only choice.

The wolves

We catch an El-Al flight. El-Al means 'up and high' in my old country, which is where we are going because my baby's grandmother has gone blind.

The morning after my arrival, Jeanette comes to our room in Jaffa to pick us up. She is unchanged from the days when I first met her: smiling, her blond hair tied back in a velvet bow. She takes us in her car to Degania Street. This is the place my mother used to clean so thoroughly that the birch veneer peeled off the kitchen cupboards, swollen with water and an excess of chlorine. Now the floor is dirty; there are clothes, dishes and boxes in disarray, and rotting vegetables in the sink.

Dora's gaze is blank, drifting. She hears my voice and says, '*Ma chérie, ma fille.*' I am still her darling daughter. 'You are here. I knew you wouldn't abandon me.'

She feels around for my baby, touches her face. 'My little girl,' she says.

'Yes, I am here,' I say. 'Everything will be all right, you will see.'

She cannot see my eyes, which are red from hours of crying.

My friend Ziva has persuaded an eye specialist at the Wolfson Hospital to listen to my story. But on hearing the word 'Wolfson', Dora says this sounds like 'wolf' to her, so she won't go to that hospital because she is a lamb and she is afraid of wolves.

'Very well then,' I say to her keeping my voice low – my baby is asleep against my chest, snug inside her pouch – 'I will fly back to Australia like a hawk and change my address like a fox. You will never hear from me again.'

She is sulking, like a naughty child. 'All right then,' she whispers, her head bowed. 'I will go.'

'Who are you?' Dora asks the doctor at the Wolfson Hospital who inspects her eyes.

'I am a doctor,' he replies.

But Dora is not satisfied with his answer. She asks me: 'Is this one an Ashkenazi or is he one of ours, a Sephardi?'

She is not, of course, the only one to divide our people into two opposed racial groups – occidental Jews, the Ashkenazim, versus those of the Orient, the Sephardim. But she pushes her discrimination a step further. 'Is he religious or secular?' she asks. When she doesn't get an answer she fumbles to touch the doctor's head, to find out for herself if he is wearing a skullcap.

Although they look annoyed, the doctors understand my case. Emotional considerations often override rules in this country. They will let us jump the queue without having slipped them a bulky envelope, because they know I haven't got any spare notes; I have flown here on charity money. And so a date is set to perform the cataract surgery that will soon restore sight to Dora's good eye.

I leave my baby with friends in Jaffa, providing a tin of powdered milk formula and silicone dummies. Dora undergoes her first medical check-up in some thirty years. She is wearing many layers of her own crocheted undergarments; it takes a long time to undress her. She complains about the cold and the nurses complain about the tight buttonholes and neck openings.

As the trolley is wheeled into the operating theatre I have to prise her fingers open to free myself from her clutch.

Hours later, she wails, 'They have blinded me!' She rips off the bandages and looks at me straight in the eyes.

'So you see, there are no wolves in this hospital,' I say.

'No wolves?' she asks me. 'How would you know – you can't see anything, you are too young. Take me out of here, don't leave me in their hands.'

The nurses tell me to go home and get some rest.

The next morning, the nurses are agitated. 'We had to arrange a private room for her because she kept the entire dormitory awake all night. She was mumbling and bumping into other patients' beds, pushing her own bed over to the window. She managed to open it; a freezing breeze blew in, and we thought she was going to jump.'

'She was only gasping for air,' I say.

The resident psychiatrist, after a short thwarted conversation with Dora, reassures the nurses. 'The whole ward will jump out the window before this woman does, so set your minds at rest.'

I answer the psychiatrist's questions. I tell her about my life with my in-laws; husband, baby and me piled in one room with all our belongings because we can't afford to rent our own place. She shakes her dark cropped hair, fixes her sparkling eyes on me and says, 'Look at me, girl. You have done your best. Don't fool yourself into believing that your mother will be happy in Australia. After she is discharged I want you to catch your plane back to Australia and return to your husband, where you belong. There is nothing else that you can do for her here. The system will look after her.'

I know the system will never be able to look after her. How can I deny my duty? I haven't met a mother as selfless as her; how could I, her daughter, be so selfish?

'Your baby is beautiful. *Bli ayin ha'ra'* – spare her the evil eye – wishes my mother when she sees her grandchild for the first time. She gives me a blue chunky glass bead, like the one she has always kept in her bag. Years ago she bought a box of them from an Arab shopkeeper in the old city of Jerusalem. 'Pin this bead on her garment,' she begs me. 'Listen to me for once.' She is blessing my baby. 'May she be healthy to the age of one hundred and twenty, amen.'

I have to beg her to let me trickle the drops into her repaired eye. She moves away, the solution drizzling on her cheeks like tears.

At the end of our last visit, my mother stands next to me as I open the car door to put my daughter in the baby-capsule. She says to me, 'I will behave well. I will sit behind you on the plane, not next to you. Behind you I will sit and I'll be quiet. Take me with you.' She is kneeling on the ground and I have to say to her, 'Please, *maman*, get up. You know I can't take you.'

I leave her standing on the footpath. She is wearing the dress she made for herself from my old pleated cream-coloured skirt. Her arms hang loose at her sides. She is smaller than me. Smaller than my baby. Just a dot in the rear-vision mirror.

Here and there

We are flying away from the day in a big aircraft. We are chasing midnight. It's the thirty-first of December nineteen eighty-seven. We will arrive in Melbourne next year.

It's night-time, and while my baby sucks the black plastic nose of her panda bear, crying for my breast, I am stacking rolls of toilet paper and bottles of shampoo on the shelves of a supermarket. In Israel it's daytime, and Dora is making a crooked doll with long dangling arms and a strange-looking face, a present for her granddaughter.

Here it is winter and I am working in a tin-roofed factory, inserting rods into a machine to make car springs, while my baby cries herself to sleep in another woman's house. Over there it's summer, and Dora is standing on her balcony, watering her plant with a jug, unaware that the pots are overflowing, water trickling down and muddying the neighbour's washing. My washing is swivelling on a Hills Hoist flying in the wind.

Here the country is in peace; we are grilling our food in the back yard. Over there, citizens are running into gas-proof shelters in the midst of the Gulf War, dreading an air raid from Iraq. Dora is calling from a public phone because her phone has been disconnected. I can hear the siren in the background and beg her to go to an air-raid shelter. But she says she isn't afraid of bombs. Only of men.

Time is lost while I work in a factory printing waratah flowers and gum leaves onto ceramic tiles, or try to sell soaps or clean other people's houses. Dora writes letters to the leaders of the world in an attempt to recover her brother Sammy's stolen fortune.

Over here my daughter says, 'When we have money, I want to go and visit my grandmother in Israel.' Dora visits the Australian embassy in Tel-Aviv, finally resigned to going through the process required for immmigration, but the rules have changed by now. The bar has been raised: sponsoring a parent requires a deposit of ten thousand dollars, a house of my own and a stable income, none of these a possibility.

While I work, mostly to pay the rent, she is lonely in her Amidar low-rent house.

One day in 1995 she rings me and says 'I don't want to live in this house any more. And anyway, if I stay here the neighbours will poison me, you know; they are paid by the bastards.'

I plead with her to stay, to let me ring the national housing company and ask for a transfer.

'*Non*,' she says, '*non, non, non!*'

'But why not?'

'Because!'

And I hear the beep-beep-beep. Her Telecard has run out of credit.

Exile

The cyclist

Early one morning I am awakened by a knock on our front door. On our garden path stands a wiry young man holding a battered, rusty bicycle. A thick towel is coiled around his neck under his hollow, unshaved face.

'*Bonjour*,' he says to me, rotating his body towards me, without moving his neck. '*J'ai rencontré votre mère a l'aéroport en Israël et elle m'a donné votre adresse.*' He hands me a crumpled piece of paper, as if he were giving me a voucher for accommodation. I read my name and my address in Dora's familiar running writing. I invite him in. He has cycled around the world and down from Sydney, his belongings stowed in a saddlebag tied with rope. While he eats fried eggs with toast and drinks tea, he offers some information about my mother, although I didn't ask for it.

'She was sitting in the departure lounge of the Ben Gurion airport with her suitcase, but you could tell from her dishevelled appearance that she wasn't a passenger. I sat in a vacant seat next to her and she asked me if I spoke French; that's how we got talking. I told her about my travels and she gave me your address for when I got to Australia. She looked very old and she was practically bald.'

How could she be bald? She always had abundant hair. It hurts me to hear him talk with such liberty about my mother, but all the same I offer him our hospitality, which he accepts with grace. He insists on pitching his tent outside, and always asks for permission to have a shower. He spends most of his time under a tree. He hasn't been fit for walking, he explains, since a road accident in Brazil when he was jammed between two cars.

Ten days later he cycles out of our lives, without a helmet, hatless on a searing hot day. Before disappearing he turns back and rides in a wide circle past the three of us for a last greeting: 'If I ever go again to Israel I'll search for your mother and tell her about you three, *Au revoir.*'

The armchair traveller

On a warm day, we dive into the ocean, the three of us. A small family tossed in the surf, each trying to catch a wave and ride it to the shore. We lie on the sand; we sit up, sandy, and eat watermelon, juice dripping from our fingers; we rinse ourselves in the cold water, shivering, then we run back and embrace the warm sand again.

It's a long drive from the ocean beach, back to the busy streets of Richmond. We enter our house, following each other in a line through our narrow passageway, and drop our bags in the main room. On the fax machine I find a page written in Hebrew. I read:

Josi, shalom, I am a security guard in the Ben Gurion Airport. As part of my job tonight I spotted an abandoned suitcase near the staff dining-room. I immediately connected the battered suitcase with the old lady who was sitting at one of the tables ... My heart was touched. You are sitting somewhere there in Australia, but do you realise? This woman is your mother ...

I ring him and tell my story. Does he believe me? Does he believe that if he tries to help my mother by alerting the authorities to her plight, she will run away from the warm airport where she shelters in winter, back to the cold streets?

Within a week, Dora rings me from a park in King Saul Street. She tells me she was suspicious of the security guard from the beginning and shouldn't have given him my telephone number. The Organisation is trying to corner her and rob her of her freedom.

Israel, my old country, the sky is your limit, with your young, tough fighters who make their living in your airport spotting abandoned suitcases, soft-hearted.

A letter from Dora

My mother is a baglady. She writes me letters on scraps of paper she has found rolling in the park. She encloses newspaper cuttings – a photo of the queen of England or a picture of an apple cake with its recipe.

This letter is written in French on lined paper in a steady hand, neatly aligned, in blue ballpoint pen.

2nd May 1999
My dear daughter,
I will tell you everything in brief. First of all, it doesn't deprive me to send your doll a bit of money. I will explain to you what money is coming in each month: on top of my social security of 1522 shekels (sometimes more) there are the monies that people sometimes give me – fifty or forty shekels, which I usually refuse, but when they insist too much I am obliged to accept; with those who don't insist, I miss out. I am honest with them, for I get a pension. Sometimes I wonder – but I am not too sure – is it my brother's money that they are giving me back? My brother Sammy, whom I would have preferred to see alive.

I have been living alone in the street for four years. Luckily

I have found a quite deserted public garden where there is water with which I can wash myself and my clothes so that I don't look like a tramp. I have got stray cats where I hang around. I used to often go to the town of Lod, where there was an Arab family to whom I would pay five shekels for taking a bath or shower in their house. But they have gone to Ramlé and I lost their new address when my handbag was stolen. I am quite a sad sight, I who always had a smile.

As far as my expenses go, they are minimal. To eat I spend no more then 500 shekels a month and on buses another 200 shekels. I was born in a big house, which belonged to us, but we were surrounded by jealous people and by the evil eye! It is lucky that none of my deceased family can see me . . .

Speaking of grievances, I will tell you about the bastard neighbour from downstairs in Degania Street, the one who was the cause of my leaving the house. This expert thief was stealing my pension: one month I only got fifteen shekels of social security in my bank account, and another month only 200. He was also stealing my water and I had to pay fantastic sums for the bills . . . He broke up my television and was stealing my electricity too . . . May the electricity take his life, amen! And when I was out he was poisoning all my food – the oil, sugar, cocoa, vinegar, everything. Finally, he disconnected the water and the electricity so I was left without water, without light, without television, without a thing. So I realised I should not stay there.

I put my most beautiful things in one big parcel. I walked down the street and met a Bulgarian woman standing by her house. I put down my parcel to be minded and when I returned an hour later I found nothing. They had stolen it. I had thrown away a lot and given away a lot, and now I was left empty-handed. Some time later they told me that it was possible to sell secondhand goods in the old railway station of Tel-Aviv, and that's how I earn some extra money now. I find nice things and sometimes I buy goods from old people's homes, and I sell them.

I won't continue to talk, even though there is more to say. I wish the three of you all the best, always health, joy, happiness and all the best.

Au revoir, big kisses to your doll.

The sisters of Nôtre-Dame de Sion

She calls nearly every week, at sporadic times. By the first ring I feel a pang in my stomach and I know it's her. The receiver has to be picked up by the third ring, before the answering service is activated.

'*Allô*, my daughter, is that you?'

'Yes,' I say, reluctant.

'Am I disturbing you?'

'No,' I say, opening my eyes to the first light of morning, or closing my book, or wiping my hands on the tea-towel I have carried with me from the kitchen. There is never a right time for Dora to ring me. Each call slices a tear in the fabric of my life.

'I am back in Tel-Aviv,' she says this time.

'Were you at the airport?'

'No, I was in Jerusalem. Last week I decided to go to Ein Karem – you know, where you stayed once in the guesthouse, in the convent of Nôtre-Dame de Sion. I got there in the afternoon and knocked at the gates, and a nun came and let me in. She gave me a meal, nice French food. I told my story to a group of the sisters and they gave me a nice room to stay in. I was so happy – finally somewhere to rest and keep clean, with large grounds, trees, birds and fresh mountain air. I was quiet like a mouse, just doing my washing or sitting in the corner of the garden. But yesterday they said that they couldn't keep me any more. I packed my suitcase and walked away, beside the beautiful stone houses. I cried on the bus back to Tel-Aviv. Now I am back in my park, in King Saul Street. What else can I do?'

'Oh, *maman* . . .'

She senses the sorrow in my voice. 'Don't worry,' she says. 'Just do what I tell you and everything will sort itself out.'

'All right,' I say.

'Do a portrait of Bill and Hillary Clinton. Listen to me, don't be stupid . . . OK?'

'Yes,' I say.

News from Israel

Dora has sent me a copy of Israel's tabloid newspaper *Ma'ariv* from the third of March 1999. She has trimmed its edges unevenly with scissors, probably to get rid of excess weight for sending it airmail. She found it in the corner of a park, I guess, because the paper is out of date and yellowed. It's folded inwards to expose the back page, which is dominated by a photo of two smiling girl-soldiers in khaki uniform, most likely from the *Hiba* street patrol. Their hair is pulled back, twisted and tied into baubles, and their faces are painted, to celebrate the holiday of Purim.

The caption beneath the photo reads: 'In the shadow of the events in Lebanon, and in the shadow of the continuing alert because of fear of [terrorist] attacks – Israel is celebrating today the holiday of Purim. Two girl-soldiers in Jerusalem are early and have already donned a disguise.'

I flip to the first page of the paper. It's been a while since I read any news from my other country. A photograph of the head of the Israeli army hugging a man in traditional Druze costume is captioned: 'The chief of staff Shaoul Mopaz with the father of one of his officers – bless his memory – at his funeral in the village of Yarka. About the funerals – see pages 4–6.' The next eight pages bear the repeated broad headline, 'A Deadly Ambush for the Commander'. There are photos of soldiers killed in this ambush, and photos of their funerals. Coffins wrapped with the Israeli flag – the blue Star of David and stripes on white canvas – are lowered into the ground by fellow soldiers. Politicians shovel fresh red earth onto the coffins, overlooked by the bereaved relatives.

In the northern border town of Kiryat-Shmonah, children have missed the Purim celebration, having spent that day inside the bunkers. The mayor is quoted: 'In this town there aren't holidays. We celebrate Purim at Passover, and Passover at Shavuot. God knows when we will celebrate Shavuot.'

On the second-last page there is a notice of mourning. A thick black line frames the photo of a young boy and a message underneath reads: 'Three years have passed and you aren't with us. Y. L., twelve-and-a-half years old, who was killed in the terrorist bombing of the Dizengoff Centre, Tel-Aviv, on the eve of Purim, 1996. And we miss you.'

I return to the back page, looking at the photos of the two girl-soldiers. The forehead of one is painted with a third eye, and the other girl's face is scribbled with whiskers and the markings of a cat. Dora has written her own caption in blue ballpoint, with an arrow pointing at the cat-soldier. Her writing says: 'I found this cat so amusing that I am sending it to you and at the same time you can read this paper.'

The kindness of strangers

In my sleep I hear the phone ringing. I pick up the receiver in the dark.

'*Allô*? Is that you, my daughter?'

I mumble a '*Oui.*'

'Are you asleep?'

'No.' If I say yes it will be untrue, now that I am awake.

'Listen, I am at the airport; I decided to come here because the rainy season has started. It's cold outside now and here I have a place to take a shower. I must tell you how I got here – are you listening?'

'*Oui,*' I say. If I listen, the call may be over before I am fully awake. In the background I can hear the calls for passengers to board a plane.

Dora continues. 'I was carrying all my belongings along Allenby Street; they were very heavy, my suitcase and my parcels. A young couple saw me; they were fiancés, you know, very decent, and insisted on carrying all my things. I was looking for a bus to the airport and they said they would search for me. The young boy went, while his fiancée stayed with me. It took him a while: all the minibuses were full, but at last he found a place in one of them and carried all my stuff there. I gave money to the driver, but the boy took the money out of the driver's hands and gave it back to me, paying with his own money, and then the girl put in my hand a twenty shekel note. I wished the young couple a long healthy life with lovely children who would be kind to them, the way they had been kind to me. They waved to me from the footpath as the minibus departed. Now I am here. At least it's warm inside.'

'Yes,' I murmur.

'*Allô*, are you there?'

'Yes . . .'

'Did you do what I asked you to do?'

I mumble.

'Are you asleep? What's the time at your place now?'

I press the clock button.

'Four o'clock in the morning.'

'Oh! Excuse me, I got confused again with the time.'

I wake up and lie in bed for a while, thinking that in New York they must have started counting the bodies pulled out of the rubble. I think about my mother, who is pulling her suitcase along looking for a suitable corner to settle in, oblivious to the possibilities of war.

The House of Courage

Letter to an anonymous judge

This fax is written in Hebrew, addressed to a judge and sent care of a social worker at the Shmuël Harofe Hospital in Israel. Number of pages: 6.

His Honour,
On Sunday 25/11/01 I learned that my mother, Mrs Dora Behmoiras, was admitted to the Shmuël Harofe. Accompanied by two nurses, she called me from a public phone and expressed her grief at being imprisoned (her own words) in the hospital. I immediately asked the nurses for the hospital telephone number.

I spoke on Monday morning with the ward matron and with my mother. The matron told me that my mother is a delightful woman and that she is physically healthy. My mother told them that she wants to get out of this 'jail' and be free.

I am writing to ask the court to release my mother as soon as possible. The only solution, as I see it, is to arrange for her a room in a place where she can be free to live the life of her choice.

Dora's story spreads over four pages. On the sixth page I write:

I am asking you, His Honour, please not to take away from my mother the only possession she has — her freedom. This is a thousand times more precious to her than a bed and medical care. I am scared that if she loses her freedom she will die within the year, because I know my mother and if one person is the symbol of freedom it is she.

They are going to take my mother to a nursing home, so the social worker tells me. It was she who suggested I write to the judge, and now she shares my disappointment. Defeated, she tells me that she had to apply for Dora's pocket money so that she could buy her daily packet of cigarettes. 'I can't tell her that she has no access any more to her pension. The poor woman would die on me if she knew.' I am shocked to hear about Dora smoking, as if this were a new sort of misbehaviour. But who am I, the deserter, to judge my mother?

Dora will be driven in a van by a young male nurse to Naharia, a town two hours away and huddled in the foothills near the Lebanese border. How will she read the landscape on the way? The Mediterranean Sea on the left, occasionally fringed by palm trees, appearing and disappearing, facing the towns, fields of vegetables, banana plantations and orange groves. The countryside hasn't changed all that much since Dora and I took this road in the opposite direction forty years ago, coming from the port of Haifa in a pick-up truck. I sat next to her, our suitcase wedged between her feet. This time Dora is clinging to a wheeled suitcase containing her few possessions and clothes, which will soon be circulating in a communal laundry, bleached and boiled into odd shapes.

Incarceration

I dial Dora's new number.

A voice answers: 'The House of Courage'.

'I am calling from Australia . . .'

'From Australia? *Oy oy oy!* I will try and get your mother quickly,' answers a female voice with a Russian accent. I hear her calling, 'Dora, Dora, it's your daughter on the phone!'

After a while Dora picks up the receiver.

'*Allô, allô,* is that you?'

I talk to her, but she can't hear me. I scream and yell, but she keeps mumbling, 'What are you saying, my daughter?' She can't form a full sentence; she mumbles. 'Two men pinned me down . . . they gave me an injection by force. *Allô?* I can't hear you.'

I close all the windows in my house so that I can cry aloud.

I keep ringing, week after week.

'*Allô?* I want to go back to Ben-Gurion Airport, where lots of people know me and love me. I am like a queen;

they give me money and food. There is a lot to see there. Here I am locked in. I have a bed now, that's all. And the food is horrible – I am not hungry any more.'

'But *maman*, you can't live like that, in the streets, for ever!'

'*Oh, là là,* how would *you* know? You think I can't live on my own, but I know I can. I am not happy here and I am the one who lives here – not you, God forbid; I want you to be a queen wherever you go.'

'Maybe I can get you transferred to another nursing home.'

'*Oh, non non.* Tell them to send me back where they took me from. They didn't ask my opinion and I haven't robbed, I haven't killed, so why am I in jail?'

Two letters from Dora

The two letters aren't dated. They were sent in one envelope bearing my address written in blue pen in unfamiliar handwriting.

In the first letter Dora's handwriting is neat.

My dear daughter,
Your letter of six pages absolutely enchanted me, especially hearing that you are making a book out of our life. I wish you success.

Above all, never send me anything; I have all I need at The House of Strength, we are housed and fed. I don't know where they get the money from, I suppose it's from my old-age pension.

Thank you for telling me I am judged special, interesting and nice by the staff here. It's very simple: I don't talk to anybody!

A few days after your letter I got the framed photo of you three – and your husband has made the frame, that's double value! So all is good and ends up well, and with a thousand kisses I close my letter, saying to you all the best.

From the mother who has only the three of you to love,
Donna

She has reverted to the name her family used to call her when she was little: Donna. Has she finally found happiness? I am filled with hope. I keep reading.

The second letter is written in pencil and on the same sort of paper, torn from as notebook, but the handwriting gets shakier as Dora's words unfold. It starts abruptly:

Above all never come to Israel, especially as this would cost a lot and anyway you will find your mother dead, for everything here tells me that I am not loved because I don't speak their language . . .

Her words trail away, shaky and illegible.

I need to see my mother now.

Reunion

'I am coming to see you next month,' I say to Dora on the phone. 'With my daughter.'

'What? I can't hear you.'

I yell at the top of my voice: 'I am bringing my daughter!'

'Ah, you are bringing her. No, no, don't bring her!'

Could it be that she knows about the terrorist attacks? But she hasn't been aware of the real world for a long time. I don't think she would know about the bombs that are exploding in buses, cafes and busy streets, randomly claiming lives.

'She is coming, she wants to see you,' I say.

'Ah, no, don't . . . This place I live in is a disgrace.'

'Do you want to see her?!' I scream.

'See her? Ah, yes, I do. But she will be disappointed. I am so old and ugly.'

When I tell my daughter what her grandmother has said, she laughs. 'My grandmother is so funny.' I haven't told her yet that her grandmother was a baglady. Now that Dora is in a nursing home she doesn't have to know the truth. Not yet.

My daughter says she is looking forward to the visit. This is what she always wanted. We are counting the days to our reunion. Twenty-two.

House of courage

We will be there in ten minutes. At nine o'clock in the morning, the autumn sun is already hot. We are walking along the quiet streets just like we used to walk together, Dora and I. The landscape hasn't changed much. Same four-storey apartment blocks, their front gardens fenced by low brick walls enclosing lush vegetation. Frangipani, hibiscus, lantana and all the other plants of my childhood. We used to walk looking up at the balconies and windows, Dora and I, thinking to ourselves, *So many apartments, they are all nice. How is it that there isn't one for us?* In those days we walked for all sorts of reasons. The main one was to escape – our asbestos hut and our enemies.

I push open the heavy glass door into the day room. I look around, scanning the old faces for my mother, but I can't see her. A nurse waves at us, saying to an old lady with abundant white hair cropped without style, 'Here she is, I told you she would come.' To me she says, 'Here you are at last, your mother was expecting you last night. She was disappointed; she thought you were not coming.'

I see my mother. She looks like a stranger. Her face is corrugated with wrinkles, her lips bunched up, and when she says, softly, '*Ma fille,* my daughter, here you are,' her mouth is a hole with just a few teeth remaining. She is dressed in a man's oversized white t-shirt and navy polyester tracksuit pants.

'*Maman* . . .' I say. I have no other suitable words.

My old mother is looking at me with her good eye, steadily. She doesn't smile. She doesn't blink. She says, 'Don't cry.'

I try to read her mind. Is she saying, *Where were you for the last fifteen years?* I am scared.

She opens her mouth and talks again. 'Don't cry. Look where I live. It's so *pashoot*.'

She utters the word *pashoot* – ordinary, vulgar – with disdain.

'How do you say grandmother in Hebrew?' asks my daughter.

'*Savta*,' I reply.

'*Savta*,' she says to my mother.

'My darling granddaughter. I love you very much . . .'

'*Savta*, I love you too.' She bends over and kisses her grandmother on both cheeks and my mother kisses her many times.

Nothing can be said; there are no tears left. My daughter and I cart three plastic chairs out through the glass doors and align them by the metal ramp that separates us from the garden. We come back and take Dora's hand. She wobbles on her feet. I can make out the shape of a large nappy under her tracksuit pants. We walk her outside and sit down. She is still staring at me. I look at her: she is small and shrunken, her chin drowning in folds of skin, but her cheeks are still peachy, if speckled. She keeps staring at me with her good eye, as if I am a stranger, and I am afraid of what lies inside her head. Will she curse me like her great-grandmother cursed her descendants? It's hard not to believe in that ancient curse now that I see my mother in this place, living among strangers.

She is about to speak, and my stomach hurts.

'I am looking at you,' she says, 'because I want to get plenty of you while you are here.'

A swarm of small flies is buzzing around us. Dora tries to wave them away, but her hand is too slow. She dozes off and we stand guard, relentlessly chasing the flies from her eyes and the corners of her mouth. She wakes up and stares at me again, and I am more scared of her than I have ever been before. Her silence pierces my soul. I want her to talk.

'How long are you going to stay?' she asks.

'About ten days,' I say.

The silence is heavy; so is the heat.

'Are you thirsty?' I ask.

'Yes,' she says.

I buy her a fizzy lemon drink from the vending machine that stands outside the day room.

'This is very refreshing,' she says.

'Haven't you had one before?'

'No,' she says, 'I don't have any coins. Ten days, is that all? It's not much. Not much at all.' She has been here for ten months. I can only stay for ten days.

A sudden shadow is cast over Dora's face. I turn around and see a doctor in her white coat. She addresses me: 'Can you please come with me. I need to talk to you.'

She doesn't waste time introducing herself. 'Did you know that your mother lived on the streets?'

Yes, I know she was on the streets. For a long time I worried about her cold nights on the bench, missing her stolen blankets. I recite my story about Dora's fear of doctors, which prevented her from migrating to Australia.

'Do you know what state your mother was in when she was picked up?'

Yes I can imagine how she looked. But how can I explain about Dora's forceful voice, which she lost the day she came to this place, and has never recovered? How can I explain about Dora's defeat?

I say to the doctor, 'Food, shelter and medicine are no match for freedom.'

She replies, icily, that they have found something wrong with my mother. Her blood cells are abnormal and something may be growing inside her stomach. She will have to be hospitalised for a check-up and possibly exploratory surgery. The doctor is giving me the choice of having this procedure done now, while I am here, or doing it after I leave.

'Can't you let her die in peace?' I ask. 'She is eighty-eight and all her life she has feared doctors. The hospital will be her ultimate nightmare, and surgery will cause her pain. Why terrorise her?'

'We are here to save people, not to let them die,' the doctor says.

When I go back to my mother she asks, looking at the doctor's room, 'What did she want?'

'Nothing,' I say, 'just to talk about Australia. She has never been there.' And I manage a smile.

The world from Naharia

It's less then ten minutes walk from the nursing home to a small cafe near the corner of the buzzing Ha'gaaton Boulevard. We sit down to a meal of hummus, falafel, pickled green chillies and turnips, salad and warm pita bread.

When my mother was living at Ben Gurion Airport, she told me that she was cleaning cafe tables and in return was given food. 'Nice food,' she said. Now they feed her a repulsive 'mixer', the processed version of the daily meal. A chicken-vegetable-rice dish turns into an over-salted mash that she doesn't care to eat.

We walk along the avenue, on concrete tiles marked with a medley of dark stains; the thickest are the evidence of oil leaks from cars parked illegally on the footpaths. Our bags are searched by a security guard at the post office entrance. We buy a Telecard to call home. Beside this modern building there is a row of phone booths, doorless and enclosed with mesh, dusty, and carpeted with discarded sunflower seed husks and cigarette butts. I imagine Dora in one of these booths, clasping the receiver and calling my name.

The hospital

When we arrive at the nursing home the next morning, we find Dora shaking continuously as if afflicted with advanced Parkinson's disease. She doesn't acknowledge us. The nurse informs me that an ambulance is on its way to take my mother to the hospital.

'We are going to take you to the hospital,' I say to Dora.

'Why hospital?'

'You aren't feeling well,' I say.

'No, I am not feeling well,' she mumbles.

We cross Naharia. It's not a very long drive.

'She is hot like an oven,' my daughter keeps saying. Our tears are streaming, but nobody stares at us. Everyone in the emergency ward is out of their depth.

'I hope she dies today,' I say to my daughter. 'I hope she dies.'

Suddenly there is a commotion in the adjacent office, separated from us only by a glass partition. A nurse is giving instructions on the internal phone. 'Prepare intensive care for a soldier who has been shot in the stomach at a bus station. Is everything ready? The ambulance is nearly here.'

Let the soldier live, let my mother die, I wish – strongly, like a prayer.

We spend most of the day in and out of the highly equipped rooms where my mother is examined. I never find out what happened to the soldier with the shot wound. And my mother survives.

At the end of the afternoon she is wheeled up in a lift and along the corridors to the end of the geriatric ward, then into a windowless room with large lockable double doors. They park her under blazing neon lights and she squints, trying to shield her eyes with her shaky hand. I find the switch and turn off the lights. A nurse comes in, switches them on and leaves. Again I switch the lights off. A group of doctors enter and one of them switches the lights on, frowning at me.

'This is my mother,' I say to them. 'Please don't hurt her. She is frightened of hospitals; she has had a terrible life, with so much suffering already. Please don't operate on her; don't torture her.'

A dark male doctor with an Arab name, and a blond female doctor with a Russian name, chastise me in their accent-tinged Hebrew. 'You are not allowed here during doctors' visiting time.'

They show me the door but I try to stand my ground.

'Get out of here!' It's the female doctor, her eyes shooting arrows.

The door is slammed in my face. When the doctors come out, they glide away from me and my questions.

Later, Dora's bed is wheeled into one of the main wards, which is shared by six patients. She starts talking. 'I am thirsty.'

I help her to drink water from a plastic cup.

'Where am I,' she asks.

'In the hospital,' I say.

'Ah, the hospital . . .'

And she soon nods off.

The next day I find my mother still lying in her bed, but when she sees me she brightens up.

'*Ma fille . . .*' she says.

I am her daughter, her only daughter. I give her a drink of water, holding the cup to her lips, and then I hold her hand.

'Where is your doll?' she asks.

'She is tired. I let her rest in the hotel.'

Dora is silent for a while, and then she says, 'I want to get out of this hospital.' She is scrutinising my face again. 'I can't remember where I live,' she says.

'At the nursing home,' I reply.

'What is it like, the nursing home?'

'It's called Beit Ometz and there is a garden around it,' I say. 'You have been living there for nearly a year.'

'A year?'

'Since January. It's October now – that makes ten months.'

She thinks for a while. 'I can't picture it,' she says.

It is the first time Dora has ever lost her memory. This is going to be harder than I thought.

'When am I going home?' she asks.

'Tomorrow,' I say.

'And when are you going back to your home,' she asks.

'In eight days.'

'That's all, your visit?'

There is so much silence between us.

'You can't change your life because of me,' she says.

'No,' I whisper.

'It's not worth it,' she says.

How can I explain to her, without filling her with bitter regret, that it was all her making, that I never wanted to abandon her? How can I prove that I didn't betray her?

'A long time ago I told you to get a visa, and then I called to ask if you had gone to the embassy. "No," you said. And why? "It was raining." I called you two days later, and asked again, "Did you go to the embassy?" "No," you said. "Don't you want to go?" I asked. And you answered, "No. I don't want to have to see the doctor." You didn't want to go.'

'Ah, yes . . . I was afraid'

I am still angry with her.

'You were very naughty,' I say to her. 'Very naughty!'

'I don't remember,' she says.

Dora's bath

Back at the nursing home, a nurse is wheeling Dora to the bathroom. My mother clings to my hand. 'Stay with me,' she says, 'at least for the shower.'

I see my mother's shrivelled body, scrunched-up, bony and pasty. She is sitting inside the shower cubicle on a plastic chair while the young nurse washes her body with precise but soft gestures, first with soap and then with a jet of warm water until all the soap is rinsed away. She helps my mother up and we see a little cake of excrement on the seat, shaped by the pressure of Dora's buttocks into a triangle, like a traditional Purim cookie. The nurse proceeds to dry her patient and dress her with a disposable nappy and clean, dull clothes. She then attends to the plastic chair.

Sweets

Every morning, as we walk towards the nursing home, my heart sinks deeper. I know my daughter is apprehensive too. We stop at the grocery shop, where she scans the shelves for some treats to see her through the morning. For Dora we buy a tub of *mualebi*, the Turkish milk pudding topped with red syrup, chopped nuts and shredded coconut.

'Do you like the *mualebi*?' I ask.

'No. It's not all that nice.'

Maybe she is comparing it to the one we used to eat from a tin dish in the Tel-Aviv central bus station. The pedlar used to give us extra topping because Dora chatted with him in Ladino.

My mother always had a sweet tooth. It could be that she connected sugar with sweet memories, like the nougat she bought every day on her way back from school in Paris during the late 1920s. She recited to me many times the words of the nougat vendor in the Marais district. His advertisement was written in thick chalk on a blackboard fixed to his trolley, and as he recited he pointed at each word with a stick:

> *Nougat / aux pistaches*
> *Garanti / sans cacahuètes*
> *J'ai dit / les trois / pour vingt sous*
> *Et au ... jourd'hui seulement*

> *Nougat / with pistachios*
> *Guaranteed / without peanuts*
> *I said / the three / for twenty pennies*
> *And o ... nly / for today.*

I know how my mother cherished all her life the words of the nougat seller, and longed for the whiteness, sweetness and neat angles of the bars arranged on that trolley in that familiar street. She remembered hopping along the footpath, pushing open the heavy wooden door and climbing the stairs to the house of her mother, father and siblings – to eat amongst them her pennyworth of sweets.

A bag for Dora

A week has passed, although our time spent in the nursing home seems like an eternity. The social worker eases the monotony by offering me some cash from my mother's small allowance, to buy something for her. I ask Dora what she would like. But she shrugs.

'How about a bag?' I suggest. 'I will buy you a handbag and a purse to hold your coins for drinks from the vending-machine.'

'Yes, a handbag,' she says. 'That would be good, I need a bag. When are you going to get it?'

'Maybe at lunchtime,' I suggest.

'Yes,' she says, 'at lunchtime.'

'We could go now, before the shops close for the afternoon break,' I say, to earn some extra time off for my daughter.

'Yes, all right,' she says. 'Since the bag is urgent . . .'

At the Akko market we buy a purse fitted with a zipper and a wristband; just the right size and design to hold Dora's coins. On Ha'gaaton Boulevard we enter the department store Hamashbir Latzarchan, 'The Provider for the Consumer'. I want to buy some 4711 cologne, but there isn't any kind of cologne available. We buy a beige-brown handbag, a cotton knitted jumper in a muted tone of cherry, and a blue silky shirt for the coming winter.

'Do you like these things?' I ask Dora, who has just woken up from a doze.

'Oh, yes, very much so.'

She puts on the blue shirt and the cherry jumper, despite the heat. She threads her hand through the purse's wristband and looks at the bag. 'Very elegant,' she says.

But she has nowhere to go, and nothing to put in the bag because the purse is attached to her wrist. At the end of the day she hands it to me. She always gave me anything new she owned, with the familiar words I hear now: 'Take it, you will get more use out of it than me.'

A train to Brittany

When I was a teenager circling wider and further away from my mother, each time I left she would ask me to chart my itinerary on paper so that she could track me day by day on her mind-map and be with me wherever I went.

Dora knows the time has come to map the route of our imminent travels.

'When are you leaving?' She asks.

'In a couple of days.'

'And where are you going?'

'We are first taking a train to Tel-Aviv, then the next day we take a plane to Paris, and finally a train to Brittany to visit Jacques and Simone.'

'Ah, yes,' she says. You are leaving tomorrow . . .'

'Not tomorrow, in a couple of days.'

'Ah. In a couple of days . . .'

We are taking another long lunch break. We travel by taxi along a quiet highway bordered with eucalyptus trees, past the kibbutzim with their water towers, farm machinery and cultivated green fields. Once I took Dora to the kibbutz at the end of the narrow perpendicular road my daughter and I are passing right now, there on the left side. One of its young members, a willowy, graceful girl I had befriended at art college, invited me several times to spend the weekend at her *meshek*, as the members called it, and on one occasion she agreed to Dora accompanying me. My mother clutched her heavy handbag the whole weekend, wherever she walked, because she was worried that her collection of biscuits and dried fruit would be poisoned if she let it out of her sight. Along the way to and from the kibbutz she would point out houses, cars, mountains or trees and offer her particular commentary – praising, questioning, criticising. Now I realise that it was the travelling she liked, more than the destination. She yearned to be on a train or a boat or a plane.

We are back at four in the afternoon. Dora is awake, looking at the entrance door and her face lights up when she sees us.

'My darling,' she says to my daughter.

'*Savta* . . .'

'My granddaughter . . .' and the customary three kisses follow.

In our silence we absorb the ambience of the crowded day room. Groans, sighs and the pleas of residents to the nurses add to the dissonance of the loud radio broadcast in Russian, the acrid smell of body fluids, of disinfectants and of heavy cooking. But none of these appear to enter Dora's consciousness. She stares at me, then nods off, and when she wakes up she stares at me again.

'Why are you wearing this shirt today? I don't like it. The other suits you better.'

'The other one is in the hotel room, drying,' I say to her, again. 'I had to wash it.'

'Promise me that you are going to wear the other one on the plane. Travel like a lady.'

'Yes,' I say, 'I promise.'

'When are you going?'

'In two days.'

'Already . . .'

I say nothing.

'Are you taking a train to Brittany?'

'Yes,' I say.

The heirloom

'I don't know what happened to her,' says the occupational therapist, looking at Dora. 'Up until a month ago she used to go every morning to the laundry to pick clothes for the day. She wanted nice garments, tops that matched the trousers in colour and in style. Suddenly she isn't herself any more. I don't know what happened to her.'

She tells me that Dora used to participate in the craft classes, at the beginning. 'She used to make things,' she says and hands me an appliqué of a flower with yellow, purple and red petals of felt, hand-stitched onto a calico cloth.

'It's lovely, I will hang it on our wall,' I say to Dora, who has just opened her eyes. She nods.

Au revoir

Outside in the corridor, Dora's neighbour has parked his wheelchair and is peering into our room.

'It's the last night,' he says to me. I nod. 'Talk to her,' he says. 'Talk to her.'

But I am lost for words.

'You are going to the other side of the world,' my mother says, lying in her bed, her knees bent because she can't stretch her legs any more.

I am trying now to recover my lost voice. My daughter is holding Dora's hand. '*Savta*,' she says.

'*Ma chérie*,' says Dora.

A blind woman is lying in the other bed, saying her night prayer, '*Baruch atta adonai elohenou . . .*'

I join her silently. I learnt these words at the religious school, when I was a child still living with my mother. All these years I have resented the worship of that merciless force. Now I am whispering the prayer, for comfort. 'Blessed are thou, our father, our God.'

Look down, great-grandmother, you who cursed your

descendants for eternity. Look down at Haim's daughter, my mother whom I am abandoning – locked in this bed, locked in this nursing home among foreigners – knowing she will wake up in the morning to the empty space left by her granddaughter and by her daughter. Look down and see how Dora utters a blessing for us (although it could be regarded as a curse): 'May the two of you live to the age of hundred and twenty, amen.'

I kneel on the floor by Dora's bed. I hold her hand and start singing to her the lullaby she used to sing to me in Paris, a long time ago: *'Do do, l'enfant, do . . .'* Sleep, sleep, child, sleep.

My mother joins me, and we sing in two voices: *'L'enfant dormira bientôt.'* The child will be soon asleep.

'These moments are very sweet for me, very sweet,' says my mother.

I am willing to wait for hours, until my mother surrenders to her fatigue, but my daughter is too distressed by this silent desperation, the streaming of my tears. I know I have to leave. I rise and she gives her grandmother three last kisses, burning with her tears. One on the forehead, and one on each cheek.

'Au revoir, maman,' I say, with a kiss.

'Au revoir,' she answers.

Epilogue

My mother is rewinding me on her line, drawing me back. Eight days after landing in Melbourne I am in Israel again, standing in the Yarkon Cemetery talking to the employees of Hevra Kaddisha, the burial society. They look at the three of us, my friends Yoram and Jeanette, and me, and are quick to assess my financial situation. The department of social services are paying for the tombstone and this is a no-frills ceremony.

They hasten the funeral into fast-forward pace. With a prayer they slash the collar of my shirt, to bestow upon me the traditional appearance of a mourner. They take us to a tin shed and wheel towards us a trolley holding my mother in a black body-bag, me leaning against Jeanette while a crude rope is untied to loosen the black material, exposing an inner calico body bag which is in turn untied and the calico swiftly lowered. My mother's face is bruised and already decaying.

'Is this Dora Behmoiras?' the undertaker asks.

'Yes, this is my mother. May I kiss her?'

But he utters a definite 'No', enclosing my mother's

body in the calico and the black body-bag. He wheels the trolley to a black van, wedging the body between the feet of men in skullcaps who have been called to make the traditional *minyam*, a quorum of ten, for the prayer (I am refused the Kaddish on account of being a woman). We sit at the front of the van, the driver racing around the circular cemetery road, jolting over humps, swerving to reach my mother's final destination via a short-cut. By the time we three mourners have alighted from the van my mother is already being wheeled off fast on a trolley, while still a few metres away I see the trolley tilted at a forty-five-degree angle to tip her into the grave. I want to yell at them: *Don't tip her like this into a hole. She is my mother.* I reach the grave in time to see the gravedigger pushing the body, my mother slightly bent to fit snugly in the hole. Grey slabs are placed across the two sidegrooves and she is covered.

'*Au revoir, ma petite maman*,' I whisper, clutching my bunch of flowers, the men's prayer drowning my voice.

I was expecting to buy roses at the cemetery, but carnations were all I could get. Superstitious, Dora wouldn't even touch one of these flowers – she said they were the flowers of mourning.

I open my eyes from sleep and feel the familiar pang in my heart, jolting me into the reality of a new day.

Dora. My mother. Is she all right?

But today will be different from the last eighteen thousand mornings of my life. Dora is gone. She has released me and I can now roam the world without the burden of her unfolding misery – her lonely days, heavy suitcases, stolen possessions, frosty nights on a bench, expiring telephone cards, unanswered letters to the leaders of the world, looming exploratory surgery. Sleep, mother, sleep. The mother is asleep, safe in her grave.

The first light of the day illuminates the waves and the long flight of steps that will take me down to the beach. It's six o'clock; the regular bathers are already arriving. I wonder if both the Calderon brothers will be there, as they used to be at this hour every day of the year, even on stormy winter days, always present to offer the few beach devotees shelter and a warm comforting drink on the kiosk veranda.

I skip down the stairs to reach the shore of the Rock Beach, which is deserted. The Calderon kiosk is still a couple of hundred metres away. I take off my sandals and start running north beside the water, on the wet sand.

There it is. I catch my breath as I approach it. The place is animated with the regulars, their voices and movements indicating with the song of a wet man, the flap of a towel, their friendship and shared history.

Nissim Calderon is carrying big breakfast plates for his customers. Of the two brothers he is the slim, introvert one. He hasn't changed much from the way I remember him when I was a child, except for his hair, which used to be sun-bleached blond and is now white.

'*Shalom,*' I say to him.

'*Shalom u'beracha,*' he answers.

'I haven't been here for a long time, I used to come with my mother when I was a child, some thirty-five years ago. She used to speak to you in Ladino. I live in Australia now.'

Nissim smiles at me. 'Yes, I remember,' he says.

He doesn't say much more; I am not sure if he really remembers. But the mere fact that I smell the sea as I eat breakfast in this place is a way of honouring Dora's life.

Acknowledgements

I wish to thank the many friends and acquaintances who gracefully accepted an earful of my writer's monologues and offered advice on matters of life and writing. Sharing my first book with all of you is my joy and privilege.

I wish to thank Mr Moshe Shaul for his kind editorial help with the Ladino citations, which are used in this book according to the Aki Yerushalim orthography. Additional thanks to: Rita Krishowski, my first teacher, for ushering me into the writer's journey, and for sending me to Israel when I needed to be there, as did Shirley Smith. Jacques and Marie-Simone Gueron, who too provided my fare to Israel on another occasion, in addition to years of support and encouragement. Dianne Simonelli, for her imagination and unlimited friendship. Marion May Campbell, for her deep insight into my work, *et pour l'amitié*. Liz Kertesz and all the associates of the Department of English at the University of Melbourne. Sally Rippin, who planted greens in my garden to feed my family, for her luminous presence. Peter Bishop, Inez Brewer, Margaret Simons, Michael Dark and the Eleanor Dark Foundation at the Varuna Writers' Centre in Katoomba, NSW, for blessed writing space and mentoring. Sophie Cunningham, for her vision, generosity and friendship. Jenny Darling, my agent, for her contagious laughter, her wisdom, expertise, guidance and, at times, her office space as well. Marion McCarthy for her witty editing notes. Clare Forster, my publisher at Penguin, for taking on my book with passion and poise. Debra Billson, the book's designer, especially for the cover. Sarah Dawson, my editor, for *thé, bavardage, conseils et amitié*, and for her dedicated work to shape the manuscript into a book.

My best friend Michael, for believing in me, and for endless support through long hard years.